Druids

A Beginners Guide To Druids

Sophie Cornish

All rights reserved. No part of this publication may be reproduced or transmitted in any form or by any means, electronic or mechanical, including photocopy, recording. or any information storage and retrieval system without permission in writing from the publisher or under license from the Copyright Licensing Agency Limited.

CONTENTS

Introduction 7
   What is Druidry? 8

Chapter 1 – The Spirits Of The Ancestors 10
   The Old Ones 10
   The Spirit of Bear 11
   Flight Through Time 12
   The Early Farmers 13
   The Megalith Builders 14
   The People Of The tribes 15
   Bards, Ovates and Druids 16

PRACTICE – Walking the Land: Exploring Your Landscape. 17

Chapter 2 – Druidry Today 19
   How is Druidry Relevant Today? 19
   Are Druids Pagans? 21
   The Freedom Of Spirit 22
   An Animistic World View 23
   The Otherworlds 24
   Walkers Between The Worlds 25
   Do Druids Worship the Sun? 26

PRACTICE – Comparative Religions 27

Chapter 3 – Remembering The Self 28
   Druidry As a Path Of Self-Discovery 29
   The Power Of The Imagination 30
   Sense and Sensuality 31
   Visualization 32
   Meditation 33

PRACTICE – The Knowledge Of The Earth 35

Chapter 4 – The Cauldron's Brew 37
   Intuition And Intellect 38
   Working In a Druid Order 41
   Alchemy And Healing 42
   The Bardic Grade 43
   The Ovate Grade 47
   The Druid Grade 48

PRACTICE **49**

Chapter 5 – Circles and Cycles 50
- The Power Of The Sacred Circle..50
- Druids Do It In a Circle! 52
- The Four Quarters And The Five Elements 52
- The Wheel Of The Year..54
- The Solar Festivals...55
- The Fire Festivals...56
- The Festival of Imbolc..56
- The Festival of Beltainne 57
- The Festival of Samhuinn...57
- The Dynamic balance of Masculine and Feminie 58

PRACTICE – Creating a Sacred Circle **61**

CHAPTER 6 – Gods, Goddesses And Beyond 63
- Do Druids Believe In God? 63
- The Druidic Vision Of The Gods 64
- The Divinity Of The Masculine And Feminie............................65
- The Loss of Connection With Our Gods....................................67
- Reconnection Through Myth And Story 67
- Druids As Ecology..68

PRACTICE **69**

Chapter 7 – Ceremony, Ritual and Magic 71
- What is Ritual?...71
- What Information Do I Need? 73
- Ceremony..73
- Magic 74
- The Mechanics Of Ceremony And Ritual 76
- Casting The Circle..76
- Opening The Four Quarters..77
- Closing The Circle 80
- Ceremony And The Eight Festivals..82

PRACTICE – Creating A Ceremony **84**

Chapter 8 – Straight Time, Curved Time 86
- Life As Linear Time 86
- Life As Cyclic Time 88
- Working With The knowledge Of The Circle 89

PRACTICE **92**

5

CHAPTER 9 – Life, Death And Rebirth 95
   Reincarnation And Transmigration 95
   The Circles of Existence 97
   The Blessed Isles 99
   The Mabon And The Goddess 100
   The Gods Of Druidry 101

Introduction

It's not hard to rediscover the wisdom of the Druids - the wisdom of those ancient spiritual teachers of the western lands. It is written in old stories, the old pre-Christian laws of Ireland, the wisdom-triadsof Wales, the folk customs of Brittany, Cornwall, Scotland and England. But even more so - it is written in the very land itself; and this book so clearly shows - we can recapture this knowledge and build on it to make Druidry a living spiritual practice that is intensely relevant to our lives today.

In the old days, the Celts and the Druids would give thanks to the Goddess and would ask for her help in healing, and in the granting of wishes, by casting precious objects into sacred wells, pools and rivers. They would take something that was of value to them and, with a heart-felt prayer, would watch it sink beneath the surface of the water, down into the depths of the Mother. Nowadays - forgetting the origin of this custom - we throw coins into wishing wells, hardly believing our wishes could come true in this way. But we still do it. Somewhere a part of us knows the power of water, of the well, of the depths. And knowing the origin of this custom helps us to understand the importance the ancient Druids placed on the Goddess - despite the common misconception that Druids used to worship the sun and were patriarchal.

Today just as many women follow the Druid way as men, and the Goddess with her consort, the God, is fundamental to Druidspirituality. Here, in this book, we discover the significance in Druidry, and we discover, too, how we can start to work with Druidry as a living spirituality that can transform our lives.

What is Druidry?

Druidry today is alive and well and has migrated around the world forming a wonderful web of people who honor and respect the Earth and the sacred right to life to all that is part of the Earth. Like a great tree drawing nourishment through its roots, Druidry draws wisdom from its Ancestral heritage. There is a saying in Druidry that 'The great tree thrives on the leaves that it casts to the ground'. Druidry today does not pretend to present a replica of the past; rather it is producing a new season's growth. The Spirit of Druidry remains constant, honoring the interrelationship of all life, whilst the face it presents to the world refreshes and renews itself continually.

Druidry is a way of life, a Spiritual Path, a philosophy; it engenders religious experience, though whether one could call it a Religion is debatable, for it certainly does not embrace any dogma. The teachings of Druidry have evolved through the centuries, and through these teachings we can find a way of understanding our own life in relationship with the world around us, and the Greater Life that flows through and gives birth to all that is.

And so in honor of the Ancestors and our own rich heritage, let us look at how we arrived at this powerful turning point as we enter a new century and a new millennium, and what Druidry means for the Druids of today.

Chapter 1 – The Spirits Of The Ancestors

So simple is the heart of man

So ready for new hope and joy;

Ten thousand years since it began

Have left it younger than a boy.

Stopford A. Brooke, The Earth and Man

The Old Ones

'Once upon a time', deep in the mists of time, before Britain was separated from Europe by the melting waters of the last Ice Age, lived a people who dwelt in an abundantly forested landscape. For thousands of years they inhabited the vast landmass of Europe; their tools of stone and flint are all that we have to mark their time upon this earth. Around 120,000 BCE a new race of people emerged that we know as Neanderthals, named after the place where their remains where found, in the Neander valley in Germany.

There is much more to be discovered about these people but

what concerns us here is how they perceived the sacred mysteries of life and death that we still struggle with today.

Their burial customs show a great reverence for those who had left this earthly life and a strong belief in an afterlife. The bodies of their dead were usually buried in graves dug in the earth of the caves that sheltered the tribe. Often they were buried close to the hearth fire. Axes, flints, flowers, food, tools of stone and bone have been found to accompany the dead. Their bodies, covered in red-ochre, were carefully laid in the fetal position with heads to the east. The red color of the ochre has signified for many cultures throughout time the red blood of life and death, whilst the east-west position of the body speaks of the life and death of the sun in its rising and setting.

The Spirit of Bear

Within other caves in Europe have been found thousands of bones of bear, laid out undeniably with a sense of ritual. At one of the caves at Drachenloch in Switzerland six rectangular stone chests were found filled with the bones and skulls of bears. In one chest all the skulls were arranged to face the entrance of the cave and by this entrance was a fire-pit with ashes which dated back 70,000 years.

By this fire-pit was an altar of bone on which rested the skull of a cave bear. The Spirit of Bear must have held great power for these people. Even from our distant vantage point we can understand the sense of sacredness of life and death that these early people must have held. The ritual care they took of the dead members of their tribe and the offerings to the Spirit of Bear would be understood and honored by Druids today. That which we speak of as Druidry, as we enter the twenty-first century, comes not just from our more recent Celtic heritage but a time deep in the ancestral memory that lies buried in the bones of the earth. From these early humans we gain a profound sense of the sacredness of being human in relationship to all that exists around us.

One of the skulls in the Drachenloch cave had around it a circle of stones. In stone and bone lives the spirit of our ancestors.

Flight Through Time

We have much to see before we reach the present day, so let's call on the powers of the shaman and take flight. As we soar above time to around 60,000 BCE we witness the appearance throughout Europe of the people that were named after the place in which their bones were first discovered, the Cro-Magnon. These people were hunter-gatherers and for around 50,000 years many tribes followed the herds of mammoth, bison, horse, antelope and reindeer, settling when vegetation and hunting were plentiful.

This period of time saw many changes in both climate and way of life. We can also witness a growing confidence in the way in which our ancestors interacted in a creative relationship with the powers of the Other worlds. The caves of Europe have, for centuries, guarded the evocative artwork of these so-called 'primitive' people. We cannot ignore the powerful magic that these paintings evoke for us even today. In their stunningly beautiful paintings there are no superfluous lines, only the essential quality of the animal is depicted. Its essence, its power, its spirit, these are what the artist invoked when she or he worked in the silent darkness of the cave, deep in the womb of the Earth Mother. It was a magical act, the role of artist as shaman. On the cave walls can be found the images of the shamans themselves. Both men and women functioned in this role, their faces masked and their bodies adorned in the skins of the animals that for them held special power. It was the role of the shaman to transcend physical reality and in consciousness communicate with Spirits of the animals. For at this time the animal world was a vital source of life to the hunter-gatherers.

From this period of time in the lives of our ancestors, carvings of bone and stone have survived speaking to us of their awareness of a sacred relationship with the Earth Mother: small statuettes of the female body, some slender, as the 'maiden' and others, known as 'Venus' figures, with rounded breasts and buttocks, showing the female body ripe with power. Unlike the paintings of the shaman, these figures are never masked and no corresponding male figures have ever been found. Inherent in the female body was the power of life and death. In the shaman we see the act of magic, in the 'Venus' figures we see the embodiment of magic. The Great Mother was the divine ground of being human.

The Early Farmers

Between 8000 BCE and 5000 BCE life changed dramatically as Britain was separated from the mainland of Europe by the melting water of the retreating ice-cap. The cultivation of crops replaced the need to follow the herds. The drama of life and death was now played out within the cyclic turning of the seasons. The power of the seed, the fertility of the earth and the changing phases of the moon's cycle were all understood to be part of the great mystery of life, death and rebirth.

The Megalith Builders

By 3000 BCE agriculture had been established and more settled communities gave rise to varying cultural identities throughout Europe and the Islands of Britain. Long before the building of the pyramids of Egypt, these various peoples responded to an impulse which led to the construction of many sites whose sacred power we can be in no doubt of today. The great long-barrows of New Grange, West Kennet and Wayland Smithy; the circles of Avebury and Castlerigg, the avenues of Carnac were all formed in stone from the bones of the earth. Great causeways and concentric circles forming massive banks, mounds such as Silbury Hill were created in the landscape. These megaliths and earthworks are testimony to a profound knowledge of the movements of the stars and planets through the heavens linked with the cycle of the seasons and the cycles of life and death. In order to complete such immense building projects a strong sense of community must have been present together with a shared belief in the sacredness of ritual. The completion of the final stage of the great temple at Stonehenge meant that whatever impulse had led to these awe inspiring creations now rested and the building work was now drawing to a close.

The People Of The tribes

It is only now, on our long flight through time, that we see the emergence of a disparate people that we know, collectively, as the Celts. Far from being one unified nation, they were autonomous tribal groups, whose ancestors had travelled long migratory paths from different parts of the world to settle in central and northern Europe. Into this vast cauldron of land poured the spirits of time and place, the Spirits of the Land and the Ancestors; and out of it was born the Spirit of the Celts. The powerful Celtic spirit was deeply rooted in the natural world and the ancestral memories. They were a brilliant, vibrant and volatile people; traders, farmers, metal workers and artists of profound skill and vision. The women of the Celts had equal status with the men of the tribes; they owned their own property and fought alongside them in battle. Their daily life was intimately andconsciously linked with the powers of the Otherworlds and it was their absolute belief in the continuation of life beyond physical death that made them such courageous warriors. Another powerful spirit was to influence and aid the Celtic love of freedom and challenge: the Spirit of the horse. Whilst living in settled communities throughout central and northern Europe the people of the Celts had bred small stocky work ponies. With the introduction from eastern Europe of faster, long-legged horses whose fluid movement made riding possible, the Celtic tribes were able to migrate from their central Europeanheartland and settle throughout most of Europe.

Bards, Ovates and Druids

By the third century BCE Celtic tribes had migrated west and settled in Gaul, Britain and Ireland. It is at this time and amongst these people that we meet our first Druids. Classical writers such as Caesar, Strabo and Pliny leave us accounts of them from the first century BCE, but as far back as the fourth century Druid philosophy was spoken of by Aristotle.

From these classical texts we know that Britain was the center of Druidic teaching, although we cannot be sure if it was its birthplace. What we can see is how it evolved from the start of our journey, way back in time, with our ancestors' intuitive sense of a continuous thread of life reaching beyond physical death and their knowledge that life exists in many dimensions. The Great Mother, the role of shaman, the sacred relationship with the animal kingdom, etc., all have been integral parts of the human story for perhaps half a million years and continue to be part of Druidic understanding as we enter the twenty-first century.

Whilst throughout this book I will use the term Druid, I am in fact referring to both Druids and Druidesses. Their roles can be classified into the three categories, which we know today as Bards, Ovates and Druids. Although these categories imply specific skills, they were, like all things in Druidry, interrelated. The Bards were poets and in their poetry and stories, recorded the history of the people and the prowess of their warriors and kings. Today we use the word Ovate but, in the past, they where known as Vates or Filidh. This class were the seers, diviners and also poets. The Druids also used the skills of divination and the information gained regulated the lives of the people. As the advisors of chiefs and kings they held great political power.

Druidic formal training spanned 20 years in which nothing was written down, but relied on a skillfully developed memory and the profound realization brought about by meditation and the study of the natural world. They wove together the knowledge of the inner and outer worlds in the consciousness of their people. As artists, poets, healers, teachers, keepers of the sacred law, philosophers, astrologers, etc., their influence was extensive.

A great deal has been written in recent years about the history of Druidry from the time of the Roman invasion of northern Europe to the present day, but from now on we will concentrate on Druidry as it exists as we enter the twenty-first century.

The Cauldron of Druidry has been brewing for aeons of time. It is rich with poetry and art, magic and healing. In the spirit of freedom you are welcome to drink deeply from its wisdom.

PRACTICE – Walking the Land: Exploring Your Landscape

We are truly blessed if we can spend time In the natural world. Taking a leisurely walk through a forest, standing by the sea on a wild winter's day watching the waves crash on to the shore, listening to the humming of insects on a warm summer day or to the sound of the clear waters of a mountain stream rushing to the sea, these are the gifts of nature. They heal and nurture us.

To spend time amongst the elements throughout the seasons can be energizing and refreshing. Just taking time to sit on cl park bench and simply watch the world go by allows us to relax for a while. For all Druids, a growing connection with the world of nature becomes a sacred and empowering part of our lives. Wherever you are in the world the spirits of the land, the trees, the oceans are there for you. Begin to explore your sacred landscape, listen to the voice of the wind in the trees, discover the wildlife that dwells in your area, and visit the sacred sites that have been honored by the people of your land. Watch and feel the changing seasons and open your senses to how the earth experiences the power of the elements.

Chapter 2 – Druidry Today

When we *get out of the glass bottles of our ego,*

and when we *escape like squirrels turning in the cages of our personality*

and get into the forests again, we *shall shiver with cold and fright*

but things will happen to us

so that we *don't know ourselves.*

Cool, untying life will rush in,

and passion will make our bodies taut with power

and old things will fall down,

we *shall laugh, and institutions will curl up like burnt paper.*

D.H. Lawrence (1885-1930)

How is Druidry Relevant Today?

Sometimes it begins with the understanding that nothing that wecan buy or any relationship that we have, any qualification gained, any food we eat gives us real satisfaction. There is an awareness of a sort of gap within, an emptiness, a 'something' that we are looking for which we find difficult to explain. We sense that life can be lived in a much more dynamic way that would allow us to feel more complete, more alive. In the western world we have explored materialism, consumerism, science, almost to the point of self-destruction and still we remain unsatisfied, unfulfilled. What is it that we are looking for? What is it that we want? What is it that we have lost?

When we become *conscious* of the fact that we are searching for that elusive 'something', like the heroes and heroines that fill the stories of the Druid tradition, we are also beginning the journey that will reveal the hidden treasures of life.

Druidry actively links us with the basic cultural pattern of the western psyche. Its teachings have grown out of a profound understanding of the 'oneness' of all life. Symbols such as the triple knot illustrate this. In a world where to be 'spiritual' dangerously denied being 'material', and to be 'material', equally dangerously, denied being 'spiritual', Druids of both past and present work with the understanding of the dynamic relationship of both spirit and matter. It is a spiritual path that demands that we 'get real' in the world. There is no sidestepping of issues that confront us in our everyday life. In fact our everyday life is our spiritual path.

Today's Druids are artists, environmentalists, joiners, healers, teachers, fathers, students, unemployed, computer programmers, grandmothers; they come in all shapes, sizes, genders and colors and from all parts of the world. They have many things in common, like the will to work together to create a future in which the children of the world grow up in safety and freedom. A world in which we honor our differences as well as all that we share. And a world in which we no longer abuse the natural world and all its creatures. But before we can heal the world, we must take care of our own healing.

Druidry today is, without doubt, a path of healing, both personal and planetary.

Are Druids Pagans?

Even today the very word 'pagan' conjures up extremely negative images in many people's minds, usually as a matter of habit rather than choice. It would be an understatement to say that Paganism has received a 'bad press' from the Christian Church and during the years that the Christian world was supposed to believe what it was told, the Church's view went unchallenged. But thankfully we now live in an age where we understand our right to question issues that affect us profoundly and make our own choices as to how we live our lives.

So what does the word pagan actually mean? It stems from the Latin word *paganus* meaning 'country dweller' and referred in earlier times to those who lived beyond the reach of the early Church. The more isolated country people continued to honor the Old Gods: of the animals and forests, of the springs, rivers and wells. These Deities were usually associated with the locality in which families had lived and died for centuries.

So what do Pagans believe in today? First, Pagans believe that everything in the Universe is a manifestation of Deity and therefore sacred. Second, that creation within the physical world requires the union of opposites, and the divinity of those opposites is understood and honored as god and goddess. The old gods that our ancestors revered speak to the pagans of today, connecting us once again with the land and our ancestors. We shall look more deeply at gods and goddesses in a later chapter, but for now the question remains. Are Druids Pagans?

Certainly those whose spiritual path is Druidry would endorse these beliefs, understanding all gods, goddesses, trees, animals, human beings, etc., as a manifestation of the one unknowable source of all being.

The Freedom Of Spirit

The freedom to choose our own gods should be the fundamental right of every human being. For the people of the Celts, the freedom of spirit was, and still is, the very essence of life. Druidry honours this freedom and a number of people who practice Druidry today weave the beliefs of other spiritual traditions into their daily lives. For our gods should speak to our soul and help it shine in the world. Whatever spiritual path we choose it should resonate with the very core of our being; like a tuning fork sounding its perfect note, we respond in harmony. A tried-and-tested path can provide 'maps' for our journey of self-discovery and hopefully with wise and compassionate guidance.

An Animistic World View

Does Druidry have an animistic world view? The dictionary states that animism means 'a belief that all beings and things such as rocks, streams and winds have a living soul', the difficulty being the word 'soul'. There are so many ways to understand this word, for example 'the seat of the personality', 'a metaphysical entity', 'the immortal element in a person', etc. Whilst these explanations can be applied to humanity, can we say that a rock has a soul? I believe that this doesn't best illustrate the beliefs that most Druids hold. Now if we use the word 'spirit' instead of 'soul' we are much nearer the mark. Druidry has a clear and profound understanding of the spirits of the rivers, the trees, the rocks, the earth itself. But not only does Druidry honor the spirits of the manifest world but it also holds a much more abstract view in honoring the spirits of time and place, the spirits of the ancestors, etc.

When we speak of spirits in this way we are speaking of the sacred essence, the essential nature of that to which we are referring. Our own spirits, as well as those of trees, rivers, animals, etc., are paradoxically both the unique, individual essence and, at the same time, indivisible from the Great Spirit which is all.

The vibrant animating spirit that flows through Druidry today owes much to its Celtic heritage, a fierce love of the natural world, the world of spirit, of the arts, and the ancestors. It is this spirit that speaks to, or resonates with, so many people today. The Celtic spirit sings to our longing for a life filled with meaning, with power and with joy.

The Otherworlds

Belief in the Otherworlds is interdependent with a belief in the world of spirit. The spiritual world, or the world beyond what we could call our 'ordinary understanding', is, for those following the path of Druidry, a realm regarded as a reality and with deep respect. As did their forebears, today's Druids understand the Otherworld to be a deep source of wisdom, healing and inspiration.

For Druids, the Otherworld is the source or the dwelling place of the gods and goddesses of the Druid tradition. Those who guard the ancient wisdom whether in human, animal or bird form can be found in this sacred place. Also known as the Blessed Isles it is the true home of the soul, where poets drink from its deep wells of inspiration and cauldrons possess the power to transform and heal. Those inner guardians who guide and teach us can be contacted in this world that lies close to the borders of our 'everyday world'. It is a place that, with training, our consciousness has access to, our understanding of life has a more all-encompassing vision and the larger patterns of life become clearer to us. As we find from those who journey there, it is a place where the real challenges of life are issued. Personal change, transformation and growth are demanded on any spiritual journey and contact with the Otherworld will always trigger our metamorphosis; but the blessings for those who journey with courage and a pure heart are without measure.

Walkers Between The Worlds

We have inherited a rich and eloquent spiritual tradition embodied in the myths and legends of Druidry. These stories are filled with the accounts of heroes whose perilous journeys take them into the hallowed realms of the Otherworld. In our more recent history we have come to understand the word 'myth' as describing at best, something of a dubious origin, but this could not be further from the truth. Myths are the stories of archetypal encounters; they hold the wisdom and in a sense the basic 'pattern' of a culture. The great mythologist Joseph Campbell stated 'Myth is the secret opening through which the inexhaustible energies of the cosmos pour into human cultural manifestations'.

Myths act as bridges between the worlds, maps to help us on our own personal journey. It is not wise to journey into the Otherworld before one understands the laws that govern there. Just as scientistsexploring the space-time of relativistic physics discovered the timeless space of a higher dimension, the Druids of old understood that the laws of our three-dimensional world did not apply to the Otherworld. In the old stories of the Druid tradition, many who had journeyed there believing their stay to have been only for a few days were confronted, upon their return, by a drastically changed world in which all those they had known were long since dead. Others who lived through lengthy adventures in the Otherworld returned to find that no time at all had passed. For those who walk between the worlds the stories of our ancestors guide us safely back to our own shore.

Do Druids Worship the Sun?

Well, I would say that Druids don't *worship* a single thing! I have heard that there are those who secretly worship chocolate, but I'm sure it's just a rumor.

The word 'worship' is loaded with such a feeling of something external to oneself and that is not how Druidry understands the many dimensions of life. We honor the sacred power of the sun, for without it there would be no life on earth. The sun is seen as masculine, sometimes known as Lugh the god of light, whilst the earth is feminine and known as the Great Mother. It is through the sacred union of masculine and feminine that all life comes into existence. Whilst we can see them in the physical sense as being external to ourselves, we understand that it is *through* them that we have existence and so we have a profound relationship *with* them. This relationship and the diverse roles that all Deity plays in our lives, Druids honor and respect as sacred. The act of worshipping something, as external to oneself doesn't best describe Druidry.

PRACTICE – Comparative Religions

Now that you have looked at some of the beliefs of Druids today, begin to compare Druidry with other spiritual paths. Do they include the understanding of the divine feminine? Does their wisdom come from the world of nature or the insight of one teacher? Do other paths believe in reincarnation? If so, what is their teaching? Are poetry, art, healing, divination honored as part of the journey? Are the animal, vegetable and mineral worlds understood as sacred in their own right? Do the people who follow these paths have complete freedom to express their beliefs? Remember all spiritual paths are there to help to awaken and nurture the needs of our Soul. They are all valid in their own right and each one of us must take responsibility for *our own* journey in life.

Chapter 3 – Remembering The Self

I praise the one

who, to keep guard over me,

did bestow my seven senses,

from fire and earth, water and air: ...

one is for instinct,

two is for feeling,

three is for speaking,

four is for tasting,

five is for seeing,

six is for hearing,

seven is for smelling ....

> Taliesin (sixth-century bard of Britain)

Druidry As a Path Of Self-Discovery

Each one of us is born into this world with our own unique potential, a sort of tiny perfect piece of the whole that we are each trying to manifest against seemingly impossible odds. Through this small book we can look at the ways in which Druidry can help us bring to birth that potential. It is a journey of great discovery, self- discovery, a journey of healing and fulfillment.

There *is* no meaningful connection with Druidry without an understanding of our sacred relationship with the Divine Feminine.

The Great Mother goddess is the matrix of all manifestation and our journey begins with honoring her presence in our lives. Throughher body, the earth, she expresses cyclic time in the form of the seasons and the agricultural cycle of the year. She is the great teacher of the knowledge of the continuing cycles of life and death that help us to understand our own creative process. By honoring the Goddess in our lives, we are dynamically re-owning our knowledge of being human. We reconnect with our intuition, our instinct, our physical body, our sexuality, our creativity, in a sacred and meaningful way. She is the fertile soil of the earth and the fertile soil of our imagination. Through a growing sense of her presence we begin to recognize the promptings of our own soul.

The journey begins with our feet planted firmly on the earth, honoring the Great Mother and the natural world that we are such an integral part of. For once we know ourselves to be part of the world of nature, the land that we live upon, the land of our birth, the lands of our ancestors and, for some of us, the lands that call to us, all become special, sacred, powerful. When we are back in relationship with the earth again, the healing has begun; we have discovered a deep source of nurturing and wisdom that has forever been our birthright.

Let's begin by remembering ourselves, putting ourselves back together again and making full use of the skills that we all possess, simply through being human.

The Power Of The Imagination

Our ability to 'imagine' is one of the keys that help us make changes in our lives. Without it we become locked into a world that fears change. We can't see how things can ever be better than they are right now. We feel trapped in painful situations and that the external world is totally manipulating our lives. Through an exaggerated reliance on the intellect we have come to view the imagination as a faculty not to be trusted or valued. How many times have you been told, 'Oh, you're probably just imagining it'? And your sense of something 'other' has been denigrated to a worthless state. Of course, we must all learn discrimination in the innerworld as we must in the world of apparently solid reality, but we can't learn it in theory, we have to *experience* the worlds where image and symbol have meaning. For they allow us a deeper insight into life. They allow us the freedom to make changes, create works of art and even a better world. When used wisely and with integrity the imagination is a powerful magical tool.

Our ability to imagine allows space for the promptings of our soul to take shape.

Sense and Sensuality

There is an old Celtic story, which illustrates the importance of connecting with the wisdom of our senses. It says: In the Otherworldly palace of the sea-god Mannanan there is a shining fountain, with five streams flowing from it. Mannanan explains the meaning to King Cormac: 'The fountain which thou sawest, with the five streams flowing from it, are the five streams through which knowledge is obtained. And no one will have knowledge who drinks not a drop out of the fountain itself or of the streams. The folk of many arts are those who drink from them both:

Living life on this earth is a sensual experience. When we dare to drink deeply from each of the streams of our five senses, we gain a knowledge that goes beyond the scope of the intellect and enters the realm of the soul. In order to gain this knowledge, we have to be fully awake in our body. It is no part of Druidry to aim for a spiritual goal that is detached from a life in the world. To be 'whole' as a human being, is to have gone beyond the illusion of a separation between spirit and matter. By honoring the Great Mother we are honoring our sensuality as a sacred part of ourselves.

It is no easy task to learn to feel again - to really feel. Our senses are the gateways to deeper wisdom, but our senses have become dulled, and many of our feelings can seem unacceptable to ourselves and those around us. In order to learn how to be fully awake to the wisdom of the body, the soul and our innate spiritual Self we need a safe space in which to work. The world of nature offers us this space - a sacred space in which we can learn and grow.

There is another sense, which we need to develop in order to work in this way, and that is 'common sense'. We could say that common sense is a powerful mixture of 'gut feeling' and intelligence. As you go through this book or join a group, whether it be of Druids or of any other spiritual path, if something doesn't feel right for you, don't do it! It may be that you need more information, so never be afraid to ask questions. If you are ever made to feel foolish by asking questions, you're in the wrong place. It is the intelligent way to gain knowledge. Sometimes certain meditations or ceremonies don't feel right for us at a particular time, that's fine, don't do them. Learn to trust your common sense. In every path of life there are those who are willing to tell you that they know what you need better than you do yourself: their egos become inflated, and they believe themselves to be some sort of Guru. But there are no Gurus in Druidry. If you meet one, run the other way! If you give some people a long robe, a drum and point a television camera at them, they somehow become directly descended from Merlin or the Lady of the Lake, Everybody has their problems, but these needn't be your problems. Trust yourself.

Visualization

This is a skill we all possess but sometimes we don't recognize it. It's the inner picture we have when we daydream or imagine the face of someone we love, or when we try to picture where we might have left our keys or the odd sock that's gone missing. For a moment (when you have read this sentence!) just relax your focus and imagine an apple, make it a red apple or a green one, let the picture fade, then imagine your front door and the handle or lock. That's it! You can do it. Visualization skills can be developed the more we allow ourselves consciously to use them and, like imagination, it is a powerful tool in meditation and ritual.

Meditation

There are many ways to meditate, but throughout this book we will use a method that consciously honors both body and spirit. There are methods of meditation that deny the body its part in our spiritual journey. In meditation our body is supposed to 'sit still and behave itself' whilst we get on with 'something spiritual'. This is not what we are going to do! Every cell in our body has consciousness; spirit and matter exist in a dynamic relationship. Time spent in meditation is the perfect opportunity to acknowledge this relationship. In effect, you are inviting your body to join in the meditation. Throughout the meditation, if you want to cough, then allow yourself to cough. If you have an itch, then allow yourself to scratch it. By listening to and acknowledging the body's needs, over time, the body becomes less demanding and we become more sensitive to the wisdom of the body. The body is matter, mater, Mother and by honoring the body in meditation we also honor the Great Mother.

So let's begin. Choose a time and a place where you can sit comfortably and will be uninterrupted for about half an hour. Take a deep breath, and as you release it, allow your body to relax. Consciously check through each area of your body starting with your forehead. Are you frowning? If so, tense the muscles even harder, then let go of the tension and let it relax. Then your jaw: move your lower jaw to free the tension, then let go and allow the muscles to relax. Next, your neck and shoulders: if you need to move them around, tighten the muscles even harder, then let go, relax. By tightening the muscles and then letting go, we bring to consciousness the difference in the feel between tensed muscles and relaxed ones. Travel down through the rest of your body in the same way. Imagine that all the tension is gently draining downwards. When you get to the soles of your feet, imagine the tension draining down into the earth. If it feels right, ask for the blessing of the earth on your meditation. When you feel ready take another deep breath and as you release it feel the whole of your body relaxed and centered. Then, in your own time, read the following passage. With each sentence, allow the images and feelings to surface. Take your time, just drift into the images and begin to connect with the knowledge that is held within the natural world and the spirit of Druidry.

PRACTICE – The Knowledge Of The Earth

Imagine yourself sitting on a hillside, resting your back againston old hawthorn tree. The warm autumn sunshine shimmers like gold on the mellowing leaves of the broadleaf trees in the valley below. But from the cool darkness of the conifer forest behindyou drift the soft chill mists of the late afternoon. The silence is broken only by bird-song, the peaceful humming of insects and just occasionally, a sharp crack, as a twig snaps in the forest. Maybe the stag watches you; he certainly roams this wild and beautiful place. In the tall reeds, spiders have woven webs that will catch the evening mists and glisten with rainbow colors in the morning light. It is the time of the autumn equinox, a time of harmony, a time of balance, when day and night are of equal length and the earth rests as the crops are harvested.

Just for a moment, close your eyes and draw from deep within yourself the feel of autumn. Take your time, recall the sound of bird-song, the smell of the damp forest, the thrill of being close to wild creatures seldom seen, the strength of the trees, the stillness. And in this stillness, if it feels right, ask the Great Mother to help you touch that deeper life, the knowledge that is written, not in words, but in the beauty of the earth, the stars, the natural world. This knowledge flows through our bodies, through our souls.

Stay with these feelings and images for as long as you wish. When it is time for you to finish, thank the spirits of the earth,the stag, the trees, etc. You can return to this place whenever you need. Now, gently move your fingers and your toes, feel yourself 'at home' in your physical body, stretch if you need to. Feel your feet firmly on the earth. You are once more in your physical surroundings.

Chapter 4 – The Cauldron's Brew

The Cauldron of the Goddess Ceridwen brewed a magical potion, which imbued the one who drank from it with great knowledge and wisdom; with insight and inspiration. If the Initiate was ready, it was the gift of understanding 'all that is', of all worlds, of all times. The 'Cauldron Born' were those Druids who had been blessed by the gifts of the Cauldron. In the story of Taliesin, the Goddess Ceridwen is said to have made her magical brew after reading the books of the Pheryllt (the Druid Alchemists), from herbs picked at precise times of the moon's phases, and boiled in her cauldron for a year and a day. In a magical moment the mixture boils over and splashes the thumb of the young boy, Gwion Bach. To relieve the pain, he sucks his thumb and of course imbibes the potent brew. Instantly, he knows all things, including the fact that Ceridwen is furious with him, and he flees for his life. Through a long chase, the Great Goddess put him through a series of magical tests, until she is satisfied that he will make good use of his new-found wisdom, and sets him free to work in the world as the inspired poet and wise teacher, Taliesin.

Rather like the search of many Alchemists to find the formula for turning base metal into gold, people in the past have speculated on the herbs that were used by Ceridwen in the story of Taliesin. But it is more meaningful to understand the language of alchemy as symbolism. The completion of the work is brought about through the union of opposites bringing forth a new and pure state, whether that be of metal or psyche. It is the union of our daily life, with our spiritual life; the union of our inner and outer realities; our intellect and intuition. It is a path of relationships, both with ourselves and others, and a great deal of very difficult, but beneficial work can be done in the relationships that we have with those around us in our lives.

Intuition And Intellect

Intuition is another of those skills, which are inherent to everyhuman being. It is also referred to as the 'gut feeling' we spoke of earlier. Intuition is a function of the right side of the brain, whilst the intellect is a function of the left. But in order to have a clearer understanding of the world we need to integrate the informationfrom both the left and right brain areas.

Intuition is experienced as a clear and direct knowing that, because it surfaces with no logical information to back it up, is often dismissedas fanciful and valueless. As children our intuitive skills are highly active, but as we get older we usually find that those around us expect us to grow out of this 'childish behavior' and start dealing with 'real life'. Such a pity, for it then takes a great deal of effort to learn to trust, once again, the powerful skill that we were born with. The information that flows through our intuitive knowing covers a broad spectrum. It can be experienced as precognition, through dreams, as ESP (extra sensory perception) etc. The intuitive right brain is in touch with information that flows from the 'wholeness' of life, where everything has its unique but interconnected relationship. In the spiritual sense it is the area of ourselves that is in touch with that elusive 'something' which we can understand as God. Because our intuitive wisdom sees the 'broader picture', we can understand the relationships between the facets of life that the intellect would identify as being separate from one another. In Druidry, intuition is valued as an important source of wisdom, and a place from which inspired poetry and art surface into the world. It allows us the knowledge of our sacred relationship with all humanity, with the world of nature and the world of Spirit. It enhances our vision of life. We could say that intuition provides us with a qualitative understanding of life, while the intellect provides a quantitative understanding.

The left-brain intellect feeds us information from life in linear time; it understands the space between things and how they logically fit together. And because it recognizes the spaces, working alone, without the benefit of the intuition, it believes the world to be made up of separate and isolated 'pieces'; a world that is made up of past, present and future; with them and us; with yours and mine. The intellect is of course a valuable human skill, that collates information, which allows us to show up for work on time, or knows where to buy the paper and paints so that we can create that inspired work of art. While the intellect allows us to function with clear knowledge of the physical world the intuition allows us insight into the deeper regions of our human existence that are in shadow to the bright light of the intellect. In our western culture we have valued the intellect highly, far more so than the seemingly whimsical intuition. The world of the intellect is a world in which we can 'prove' the existence of things, problems can be solved and verified by others; we feel to be on safe ground. The laws of 'cause and effect' can be worked out and we can all agree that if we add two and two together, we will get four; or if I drop a glass vase from a great height it will break. Intellectual knowledge gives us a sense of being in control of our lives and the world around us, whereas the underlying shifting patterns of life that the intuition detects, gives us a sense of chaos that we can no longer control. There is a sense of darkness and the unknown dwelling in the realm of intuition, a feeling of a greater power at work that we, as human beings, cannot control and so we fear it and avoid it as best we can. This deeper, darker realm of the intuition has come to be associated with the feminine, and as we in the western world developed our intellectual skills, all that was linked to the feminine and the darker, unknowable (as far as the intellect was concerned) aspects of life became something to be feared. We learned to deal with this hidden side - or so we thought - by either trying to deny its existence, or naming it as evil and avoiding it out of fear of damnation. The Goddess no longer existed; seership and divination became the work of the devil; intuitive healing and magic were witchcraft; the Spirits of the Ancestors became malevolent ghosts; and death was to be feared. All this, because we denied the value of our intuitive skills.

But maybe we can understand this, not as a failure of our western culture, nor place the blame on Church or State, but instead look at the possibility that over the last two thousand years, we in the West had a particular path to tread. That intuitively (ironically), we followed the path of the intellect, whilst many cultures in the East followed the path of intuition. Whilst in the West our focus was on technology and outer space; in the East, particularly in Buddhism, the focus was on spirituality and inner space. From this point of view it appears that we have a lot to learn from one another. We can share our vast knowledge of being human. This doesn't mean that we have to imitate one another; rather we can help and support each other on our collective journey to wholeness. We in the West once used skills and had intuitive insights that for generations we have denied, but many Eastern cultures have retained anddeveloped them. There are cultures that could benefit from the technology that we have developed, and with our wise supportcould avoid many of the dangerous pitfalls of our scientific discoveries. At this important time in the story of humanity, whether we consider ourselves to be Druid, Christian, Buddhist, Pagan or the follower of any other spiritual path; we can begin to work together, stand back a little from grievances and our well-defended points of view, and begin the millennium in a spirit of co-operation.

In Druidry we consciously work towards a greater understanding of life and the world that we are part of, through the integration of the knowledge of the intellect, and the wisdom of the intuition. This work towards the marriage of intellect and intuition, of God and Goddess is an alchemical process. From this sacred union, the Mabon is born; the full and sacred potential of each human life.

Working In a Druid Order

There are many Druid Orders around the world today, each one with its own distinctive 'flavor' and way of working. The largest Order is the Order of Bards, Ovates and Druids (OBOD); which is based in Britain. You can find more details of this Order and other groups in the last section of this book. OBOD is a teaching Order with members and groups throughout the world who follow a tutored, distance learning program, it also runs workshops and retreats, which are held in many countries. As it is the Order to which I belong, and therefore have direct knowledge of, I'll tell you a little of the work of this particular Order.

Alchemy And Healing

Druidry has, woven within its wisdom, the knowledge of the alchemical process, and if this is our path then this is what we will find there. The Goddesses Brighid and Ceridwen are both guardians of alchemical knowledge, and it is to the Goddess that we must turn in order to begin the process of transformation.

The motto of alchemy was *Solve et Coagula,* dissolve and coagulate. In order to bring the alchemical process to completion, that is; in order to reach the wholeness of being human, fully awake upon this earth and using our full potential; it is required that we first look at, and understand every part of ourselves in order to bring about the integration of our total being. We can understand the base metal that alchemists speak of, as the self that we know ourselves to be at the beginning of our spiritual journey. The completion of the work comes when, in the language of Druidry, we give birth to the Mabon that dwells within each one of us. That glorious shining child of the God and the Goddess, spirit and matter, working within the world for the benefit of all life. It is a long and difficult task that requires great commitment. But when the need arises and our soul prompts us, there is no ignoring the call.

It is the call to service in the world that brings many people into Druidry, and the way we will each best serve, is through the development of our own unique skills and innate wisdom. As our spiritual journey progresses, the understanding of the need to clear away all that hinders us on our path to wholeness becomes increasingly evident. All the old habitual patterns that we have developed for one reason or another, and now no longer serve us well, can be offered to the cauldron. No matter how difficult it is to let go and change, all that we let go of will become part of the potent brew that will eventually provide us with insight and wisdom. Nothing will be wasted, everything that we have experienced in our lives, no matter how painful, will become a valuable part of our enlightened Self. We can offer it to the cauldron of the Goddess in the knowledge that it will be a step towards our own healing, and through our own healing; we can work with others towards a greater healing in the world. Whether they are poets, gardeners, fathers, priestesses, bank managers or a whole host of other ways of working in the world; the vision and aims of people in Druidry today are rooted in healing, in the widest sense of the word.

The Bardic Grade

The work of separation that we spoke of earlier begins in OBOD, in the Bardic grade with the understanding of the circle and the elements. The circle can be used as a metaphor for the self, and the elements as the facets, which represent the various parts of ourselves. In order to look more closely at how we understand and make use of the elements of ourselves, we begin by separating out these various parts.

Earth can represent our body and our physical environment,

how we nurture ourselves and one another. When we feel comfortably 'at home' in our body, the senses can be finely attuned to the rhythms of the natural world, and the world of nature then offers us great insight into the mysteries of the Goddess. It is in the realm of earth that we connect with our practical skills and maybe for some of us, our stubbornness. In the realm of earthwe are in touch with the sensual world, our bodily knowing. The senses can connect us to our intuitive skills. How much do you trust your intuition? Do you listen to your body's needs? Or do you override its messages and push yourself beyond your physical limits? Do you respond to your body's need for rest or exercise or a healthier diet?

By working with the element of earth we can look at how well we are able to manifest our skills in the world, whether our ideas and visions remain in the lofty realm of air, or whether we are able to bring them to birth in the world, to ground them. In order to begin our journey of transformation we need to be fully grounded in the world of reality, the world of spirit is no place for someone who doesn't have a sound grasp of 'the here and now'. If we can't get to grips with what the world offers us on a daily basis, there is little chance of dealing with the more subtle realms of life. Earth is our home, the physical reality that we all share, and it is the safe place to start our work.

Water is the element that connects us to a deeper understanding of our feelings and how we give and receive love. The way that we describe feelings in our culture suggests the fluid watery element. Do you bottle up your feelings? Do they overwhelm you? In the deep well of your feeling nature is great wisdom. Is the love that you have for others hidden in this deep well of feeling? Do you love yourself? This can be really hard to do if you have never felt truly loved in your life, and it takes great courage to look into the hidden depths and learn to love yourself. But as Druidry is firmly rooted in the world of nature, the path to healing can be found through beginning to open the heart to the love that exists in the world around us; the animals, the trees, the plants and oceans, the crystals and the wild open moorlands. The animals that many of us share our homes with give their love unconditionally. Many people feel real and deep love for the trees that share our planet, their strength and support is given freely.

Water symbolizes one aspect of the feminine, and it is in the waters of the womb that we have each begun our journey in this life. It was hopefully, deep within this safe watery darkness that we first experienced love from our mother, and it is to the Great Mother that we can turn for love and healing when life has been harsh and painful. Without water there would be no life on earth, without honoring the feminine, the earth would become a barren wasteland.

The element of air represents the intellect, our thoughts, ideas and visions. This is an area of that we have placed great dependence on in our western culture. As intellect is associated with the element of air, it is no coincidence that we have elevated the intellect to a lofty status. We have seen it as a higher mode of understanding the world we live in. But the more value that we placed upon it, the further we drifted away from our connection with the realms of feeling and intuition. When a person is dominated by the intellect they canseem cold and uncaring. They can live in a world of ideas, detached from their own feelings and feelings of those around them. How well do you integrate your intellect with your feelings? Does your head or your heart rule? Do you endlessly gather information through reading and training programs? Do you make use of what you have learned? How well can you articulate your ideas and insights? If you begin a project, do you generally complete it? Working with air allows us to rise above a difficult situation and see another point of view. Begin to look at how the element of air works in your life.

The element of fire represents the will, creativity, passion. We speak of people having a fiery temper, or tempers flaring. It can be associated with anger, high spirits, and willfulness. It can be dynamic, inspirational and transformative. But when it is misused or suppressed it can be destructive. Because of its ability to suddenly flare up, out of control, it is an element that many people find difficult to work with. As children we learn very quickly that fire is a dangerous element, but are very rarely taught how to work with it wisely as a psychological element. The power of fire can bring great changes in our lives when we learn how to skillfully work with it. Our early human Ancestors were familiar with the natural elements of earth, air and water, but fire was the last element that they came to understand. Fire is present in the angry words that destroy a friendship, and in the warm glow of a hearth that draws a family together. When we feel anger it is a signal that something is wrong in our lives, it is a natural feeling, but that which has triggered our anger may not be the real cause. When we start to work with fire we may begin to unearth some long held resentments. We may also release an empowering ability to be creative in the world. Do you work skillfully with fire in your life? Can you express your anger when you feel it? Is your anger destructive in your relationships? Do you long to be creative, but feel you have no talents? Look at your own life, and recognize those things you have created. Do you feel yourself to be dynamic or reserved? Do you make good use of your fiery qualities?

The work with the elements that begins in the Bardic grade is carried out through ritual, meditation, contemplation, discussion and application in our daily lives and, in the tradition of alchemy, we repeat the process over and over again. Work with the elements is combined with developing the skills of the Bards; poetry, storytelling, arts and crafts, music and song. The Bardic grade provides a rich and fertile ground in which creativity can develop, there is no requirement of excellence, just a freedom to grow.

The Ovate Grade

When the time is right, and if they choose, the Bard becomes an Ovate. But as Druidry doesn't work in a linear way, there should be no sense of leaving the Bardic skills behind; instead it is a case of adding on the skills of the Ovate.

Whilst we live in the physical world we will always be working with the elements, widening our knowledge, developing our creativity; it is a lifetime's work. What is required before a Bard becomes an Ovate, is that she or he has a firm grounding in the real world and the work of the Bardic grade. The realm that the Ovate enters is the realm of the natural world and the world of Spirit; the normally unseen world that lies beyond the apparent world. It makes good sense to be fully grounded in the physical world, with a clearer and deeper understanding of ourselves, before we enter the more subtle realms of existence. The work of the Order of Bards, Ovates and Druids is to guide people safely along their spiritual path. The Ovate grade is where the skills of divination and healing are developed, and the work of personal transformation is continued by adding to and deepening skills already gained. There is no time frame in which any of the grades must be completed ... it takes as long as it takes. There is no rush, because in fact, there is nowhere to go. We already have everything we need right here, right now, it just takes time and effort to remember who we really are, and what we have to offer to the world. By trying to hurry our journey through the work of the grades, we deny ourselves the opportunity to grow. But, no matter how long it takes, when the Ovate is ready, he or she, if they wish, becomes a Druid or Druidess.

The Druid Grade

The work of the Druid grade is the work of the philosopher, the teacher, and the magician. There can be no real magic unless the inner worlds and the outer worlds align, and the magician has the insight and the ability to direct his or her will for change. This requires great skill, and if it ist o be carried out for good, great humility in the presence of the powers of God and Goddess. The will of the magician is offered up to a higher power, and it is only by a tremendous amount of personal effort that powers can safely flow through the magicians will for change. In order to perform an act of magic that is beneficial in the world, the magician must have cleared away much of the personal debris that has been accrued in his/her lifetime. This is a tall order, and in no way discounts the magical acts performed daily by people around the world simply through the power of unconditional love. I need to speak personally now, and have to say that as we come into a time when esoteric teachings are to be bought for the price of a weekend workshop, or a simple book on magic, we run the risk of destroying the gifts that are our human birthright. As human beings, we are magical beings, able to create the world around us. As we move into this new century, let us not abuse our new-found power, but work carefully, without haste, clearing the debris of our collective past, until we can work magically and in harmony with the Greater Power that dwells throughout the many worlds of existence, and bring to birth a world that is filled with love. It is a long and difficult journey that we take, when we first step upon the path of Healing, but we can take it together, and pass the gift of our 'wholesome' wisdom on to our children and our grandchildren. Together we can work towards a world where humanity knows its kinship and honors each individual's unique and rich expression of Life.

PRACTICE

As you read through this chapter there were many questions asked. Read through the questions again, write them down and also your answers. Add the date and any circumstances in your life that you feel maybe relevant. Whenever you feel the need, read through what you have written and add any changes that have taken place and the insights that led to your change of perception. By working in this way you can begin to see how you respond to life, how life teaches you, and how you continue to grow and change.

Chapter 5 – Circles and Cycles

In the middle of a field stands the Wisdom Oak

Its trunk is a wooden rock face.

Its inside is hollow and sheltered.

Kicking and pulling I work my way up.

I reach out to touch the clouds of silver fleece,

And loose grip. I fall back to the dew wetted grass.

One thing on my mind touching the clouds again.

Bryn Fisher, *The Wisdom Oak*

The Power Of The Sacred Circle

Let's do a short visualization. As you read, simply let the images surface: Imagine yourself standing on the earth, surrounded by a circle of stones. In the east, just rising above the rim of the worldand the eastern stone, is the early morning sun. Its shimmering rays of light gently warm the earth. Take your time, welcome the sun; it is the beginning of a new cycle.

As you watch, the sun climbs towards the south and as you turn to face the southern stone, the sun's brilliance is reflected like a million tiny rainbows from the crystals embedded in the stones of the circle. Stretch your arms to the sun and feel the whole of your body glowing with shining light.

The sun continues its journey, descending towards the Blessed Isles beyond the western horizon. As you turn to face the stone of the west, the sun's fiery amber glow rests for a moment on the western shore. Its golden warmth touches your heart and the blessings of joy and love are yours.

The last glimmer of light fades into darkness as you turn to face the northern stone. The dark indigo sky is alive with stars and a full moon casts a pale silver light on the great stone of the north. There is great power and beauty in rich dark night and the ancient wisdom of the moon and stars will guide you through the darkness. Turn once more to the east and offer your thanks to the spirits of the circle.

Allow the images to gently fade and if you need to, stretch yourbody, place your feet firmly on the earth and know yourself to be fully present in the physical world. And when you're ready ... read on.

Deep within the still center of my being

may I find peace.

Silently within the quiet of the Grove

may we share peace.

Gently within the greater circle of humankind

may we radiate peace.

Druids Do It In a Circle!

Druidry evolved in areas of the world where the daily cycle of night, dawn, noon, dusk and the cycles of the seasons were well-defined. These cycles continue throughout our lives. Circles and cycles describe our experience of life. The turning wheel of the year, the rotation of the planets around the sun, the spiraling galaxies, all speak in circles. Some of the oldest rock carvings on earth depict circular images such as spirals and concentric rings that must have held deep meaning for our Ancestors. The building of such magnificent sites as Stonehenge illustrates the importance of the symbol of the circle. When we stand together in the sacred circle of a Druid ceremony it is also a statement that everyone is of equal importance. We stand together, 'heart to heart, hand in hand...'

The circle symbolizes the totality of the self, the whole, potent, creative self. It also symbolizes the cosmos, the infinite one-ness of all life. In Druidry we honor the circle as a sacred place in which we can work, to gain a greater understanding of ourselves in relation to all that is. We could say that the wisdom found within the circle is the foundation of all Druid teaching.

The Four Quarters And The Five Elements

It may be helpful to have paper and pen handy while you read this. Draw a circle and jot down anything that 'speaks' to you as we go along. Use the illustration for reference. At the end of the chapter you can begin to create your own sacred circle but, for now, just make notes.

The teaching of the circle in Druidry is similar to the 'Medicine Wheel' of the Native American people. But as it has grown out of a different part of the earth the teaching differs accordingly. Druidry responds to the spirit of place, just as the Native Americans do.

The circle is divided into four quarters: the north will be seen at the top of the circle, the south at the bottom, the west to the left, the east to the right. It is how we view the world. As we have experienced in the visualization, we are following the path of the sun.

In the east is the dawn, the place of first light. It speaks of new beginnings, birth, youth, a new way of seeing, vision, clarity. It is the wind that brings change, the air, the intellect. It can be understoodas masculine, not necessarily gender-based, but the masculine principle. The color of the east is yellow. It is spring.

In the south is mid-day, the sun at its height, fire, heat, the fertilizing power of life, inspiration, creativity, potency. It is the time in our lives when we are 'making our way in the world', creating our own lifestyles, which may be very different from our family's. It is a time of raising our own children and our own careers. It, too, can be understood as masculine. The color of the south is red. It is summer.

In the west is time of evening, the place of the setting sun. It is a place of calm and the deep well of wisdom that maturity can bring. It is water, a time of reflection, of intuition and if we weave it with the vision and the clear intellect of the east and the experience of life from the south, then the wisdom of the well will bring a deep healing to ourselves and those around us. It is the place of the Blessed Isles, the gateway we take when we leave this world. The west can be understood as feminine and as with the dynamics of the east and south we can understand it more easily as the feminine principle. The color of the west is blue. It is autumn.

In the north is the dark cold night. The place of death. A place of the moon and stars and the deep and silent earth. It is introspection, a time of stillness and rest. It is the solid, material, earthy quality of life, the power of the manifest world. The north can also be understood as feminine. The color of the north is green. It is winter.

As we have seen, the four quarters of the east, south, west and north correspond with the elements of air, fire, water and earth. The fifth element is spirit, which flows through and is at one with all life. Its place can be seen as both the center and the circumference, it is above and below, flowing through all worlds, all times, all space.

The Wheel Of The Year

We have much more to see. In order to gain a richer understanding of life the wheel of the year is now divided or, more correctly, understood in eight sections. Between each season of spring, summer, autumn and winter, lies another marker in time, allowing a greater insight into life and giving us the eight festivals of the Druid year.

The Solar Festivals

There are four solar festivals in the Druid year.

Spring

In the east is the festival of Alban Eiler. Alban is light and Alban Eiler is the light of the earth, a time when new life clothes the earth in the new growth of spring. It is the time of the vernal equinox, a time of balance when day and night are of equal length. It is the time of the youth.

Summer

In the south is the festival of Alban Heruin, the light of the shore, the summer solstice, the time of greatest light, when life of the earth is shimmering in the heat of the summer sun. A time of union between earth and sun, when the power of the sun is at its most potent. It is the time of the sun god.

Autumn

In the west is the festival of Alban Elued, the light of the earth, the beginning of the harvest, when the crops are ripe and the sun's power is waning as this year's growth is gathered in. It is the time of the autumnal equinox. Once more light and dark are equal, a time of harmony and balance. It is the time of the wounded king.

Winter

In the north is the festival of Alban Arthuan, the light of Arthur, the time of greatest darkness, when the sun's light seems to have almost deserted us and the nights are long and cold. The earth rests and no life is seen to grow from the frozen ground. But from deep within this darkness we glimpse the return of the sun, at the time of the winter solstice. New life is germinating in the dark womb of the earth. It is the time of the sun child, the Mabon, the once and future king, Arthur, as he awakens from his long and healing sleep.

The Fire Festivals

The four festivals that are linked with the feminine principle are known as the Fire Festivals of Imbolc, Bealtainne, Lughnasdh and Samhuinn (pronounced, *Imolc, Beltain, Loo-na-sa* and *Sow-ain*).

The Festival of Imbolc

Halfway between the winter solstice and the vernal equinox, it falls at the very beginning of spring, when the first shoots begin to push through the hard, cold earth. Snowdrops are one of the first flowers to appear and these are used as a central focus in the Imbolc celebration. The first lambs are born and the days begin to lengthen. There is more light but no real warmth. The fire is very gentle at this time, just a candle flame. The earth is bringing to birth a new season's growth. This is the time of the maiden.

The Festival of Beltainne

Halfway between the vernal equinox and the summer solstice, it falls at a time when the fertility of the earth is clearly seen. Trees are in blossom and await insects and the gentle summer winds to pollinate them in order to produce the crops of autumn. The days grow longer and the newborn of many species play in the early summer sunshine. The animals are taken to their summer pastures and in days gone by would have been driven between the two Bealtainne fires to cleanse them. The power of life is potently felt; sexuality and union are honored at this time. The fire is blazingand its flames energizing life. This is the time of the mother.

The Festival of Samhuinn

Between the autumnal equinox and the winter solstice, it falls as the gathering darkness heralds the sun's light sinking into the deep dark earth. The crops of autumn have been brought in from the fields and the seeds of future generations have been swallowed up by the moist fertile earth. Samhuinn has links with Bealtainne across the circle. Samhuinn is a time of clearing and fertility; Bealtainne is a time of cleansing and potency. It is a time in Druidry when we 'take stock' of our lives throughout the year that is now drawing to a close and consciously and ritually let go of all that is no longer helpful in our lives. The Druidic saying that 'The great tree thrives on the leaves it cast to the ground' is applicable here. Just as the dead leaves fertilize the sapped earth, we can draw wisdom from those things in our lives that no longer sustain our life's needs, whether they be perceptions of life, habits, even relationships, we look at all of it. Everything has its value. It is a time to look at the lessons that our own life is offering us, to help our future growth. But it is not an easy time; it takes courage to look into the darkness of the discomfort in our lives, but all we have to do at this time is recognize the problems and consciously decide to let go. This is the time of the crone.

The Dynamic balance of Masculine and Feminie

The solar festivals are understood as masculine. They honor thegods and the masculine principles in life such as logic, intellect, the fertilizing power of life, heat, sun, light, the seed, the sword, etc. The fire festivals are understood as feminine and honour the goddess inall her forms. The principles recognized as feminine are intuition,lateral thought, cold, night, the cauldron, earth, the cave, nurturing,etc. It is quite obvious that the masculine principles are notexclusively found in men, just as the feminine principles are notexclusively about women. Whilst we can understand ourselves asmen and women to be 'specialists' in certain areas, such as ourunique roles in the ability to create children, women possess clearintellects just as men possess the powers of intuition and womencan wield the sword just as men can nurture.

One of the aims of Druidry is to bring to full potential and use wisely *all* our gifts. It is this dynamic interplay of these two forces, which are alive in each human being, that we see woven into the wheel of the year in the eight great festivals of Druidry. As we begin to consciously connect with the meaning of the cycle of the seasons through these eight markers in time and space we gain a growing knowledge of ourselves and how we 'fit in' to the greater scheme of things. We have a wider perception of life and its shifting patterns; we no longer stand in one position and have one fixed view. We can move around the circle and view life from any angle we choose. Change in our lives is no longer something to be afraid of; in fact, itis the only thing we can truly rely on. Everything in the Universe is in a state of change, playing out the dynamic dance of Life. But whenwe have connected ourselves back into natural rhythm of this sacred dance we no longer feel that we are at the mercy of forces outside ourselves. Until we can, in a state of enlightened consciousness, view life from the centre and paradoxically from every part of the circle at the same time, this work is never really finished. It may take us all a little while!

But if in your thought you must measure time in *seasons, let each season encircle all other seasons,*

And let today embrace the past with remembrance and the future with longing.

Kahlil Gibran, *The Prophet*

PRACTICE – Creating a Sacred Circle

Earlier in this chapter I suggested jotting down any ideas or information that may have spoken to you. Don't worry if you didn't, but in this practical exercise you can begin to create a sacred circle based upon all that we have looked at. This act of creation can last the whole year, longer if you wish. It is your circle and can be created in any way you choose. The basicshape is of course the circle, divided into eight sections and from there on it's up to you! I'm sure you will have lots of ideas. You could construct it from stone - small pebbles will do, it needn't rival Stonehenge! You could paint it or use collage or tapestry. A simple drawing with crayons will make just as sacred a circle as a massive work in oils. It is the spirit in which the work is carried out that weaves into it the sacred meaning. You can fill this circle with whatever feels appropriate to the section you are working with, just color if you wish, or symbols that convey the meaning of that particular time of year, or the particular period of your life.

As the wheel of the year turns, you may wish to place on the relevant section something that is special at that time of year, for example, snowdrops at Imbolc or apples at the autumn equinox. Be careful at Bealtainne! A little May blossom may be safer than a blazing bonfire.

However you create it, the circle is yours to begin the work of reconnecting to the wheel of the year. At each festival time it would be helpful to take time to go out into the natural world, a park, the countryside or a garden. The very act of consciously taking time at these points of the year to connect with the natural world is a sacred act. Whilst you are out there, really look at all that is around you, the trees, the animals, birds, the sky and the shifting clouds. Feel the wind and listen to its voice as it blows through the trees, feel the sun or the rain upon your skin. Be open to all that your senses are telling you and, when you come home, you may have another-gift for your circle, an insight that you've had or maybe a stone or a feather. There will be no need to seriously search for something; the world of nature is generous, so just relax, enjoy the freedom and see what it offers you.

CHAPTER 6 – Gods, Goddesses And Beyond

Our birth is but a sleep and a forgetting:

The Soul that riseth with us, our life's Star,

Hath had elsewhere its setting,

And cometh from afar:

Not in entire forgetfulness,

And not in utter nakedness,

But trailing clouds of glory do we come

From God who is our home.

William Wordsworth (1770-1850)

Do Druids Believe In God?

Everyone who holds a sense of something greater lying beyond their normal view of life will experience that greatness in his or her own way. The Christian Church calls that greatness God, and the Christian experience of the world flows from how they view this god. The Christian god is seen as male and somehow 'out there', and external. They would understand god as good and everything bad to be the work of an opposing force, which they name as the devil or Satan. It is a dualistic perception that can separate and divide life into opposing camps. God is out there and is spirit, while matter is down here and has to be redeemed. Druidry does not hold this dualistic view nor the sense of divinity being external to the world. In Druidry life in the physical world is the manifestation of the union of spirit *and* matter. The work of bringing this sacredunion into fully realized consciousness within ourselves and truly living it in the world is the path of Druidry.

Therefore Druids hold the understanding of ultimately the one unknowable source of all being, that in fact we have no *one* name for, though it has been called the Great Spirit, Ceugant, the source. This source flows through everything there is, in all worlds at all times. It is that which is beyond our human understanding but in no way separate from us for we are 'of it'. It is the divine power of love and life that even death is part of. Death is change, it gives birth to new life.

The Druidic Vision Of The Gods

From the unknowable source of all being we travel in consciousness to that which we *can* know, the archetypal powers that we know as gods and goddesses. Many cultures have vast pantheons of gods and goddesses. Both the Egyptians and Hindus gained a profound understanding of life through their sacred relationship with their gods and goddesses, as did the Celts and Druids. The roles of these Deities shift and change and often seem paradoxical: a goddess of destruction can also be one of nurturing, making simplistic categorizations meaningless. If we study the deities of cultures around the world we find similar archetypal forces being expressed through the cultural consciousness of individual groups of people. The gods and goddesses have a reality and through reading their stories in myth and legend we come to understand the greater forces at work in our lives.

In Druidry we work with not only the more subjective understanding of gods and goddesses but Deity manifest in the natural world. Goddesses of wells and rivers, spirits of the trees and stones, gods of the animals and the sun. We also honor Deity in each human being.

The Divinity Of The Masculine And Feminie

The path of Druidry is one of equality, not just between male and female but of all life, the forests, the oceans, the animals, everything. If Deity flows through all life, how could it be otherwise? But for now we are going to look at the roles of the masculine and feminine principles.

For so long we have, in the west, been given the vision of Deity as masculine and it has caused such trauma in the world that we can no longer function in harmony with one another. This teachingsaid ... 'if God is male, then everything that is attributed to the masculine principle, such as intellect, spirit, sun, light and men, also is good and to be held in reverence. God is not female, therefore everything attributed to the feminine principle such as intuition, matter, body, moon, darkness and women is, to put it mildly, second rate'. Now this view doesn't exactly help a world that is striving for peace and harmony because, as we all know, the feminine is alive in men as well as women and it meant that men had to deny much of what was their true and sacred selves. Women it seems had to deny practically everything. Thankfully times change and the century that we are about to leave has seen an enormous resurgence of the power of the divine feminine. As it arose in the consciousness of the western world primarily through women because, as women they actually embody it, it caused huge problems in society. The Suffragette movement at the turn of the twentieth century, the staunch feminists of the 1960s and 1970s, and the recent struggle of women in the Christian Church whose vocation is that of priestess, have all been met with enormous resistance. Change can be frightening. The sad thing is, that as we travelled through our journey in time and looked at the way Druidry has evolved to the present day, we can see that this split between masculine and feminine, whether it be Deity or human, never existed until the time when the power of Rome sent first its troops and then its priests. The indigenous spiritual tradition of northern and western Europe honored gods, goddesses and all life as the manifestation of deity. In Druidry we work with that tradition, it speaks to us through the stories of our Ancestors, through our souls and through the lands itself.

The Loss of Connection With Our Gods

When a culture loses its connection with its own gods then it truly loses its way in the world. Of course, we can 'make do', create other gods to replace them, such as money, status, designer lifestyles, etc. The trouble is that none of these really satisfy our hunger. We always need more. We have become disconnected from that elusive 'something' that gives our lives *real* and *satisfying* meaning. Getting back in touch with the old gods doesn't mean becoming 'wonderfully spiritual'; it means reclaiming the basic pattern of life, the map. When we have lost the map, we've lost our way. In the myths and legends of the Druid tradition we find the archetypal stories of gods, goddesses, heroes, wise-women, fools and warriors. They speak to us of spiraling patterns of life and, through their stories; we can understand our own unique story. Connection with our own gods empowers us; for it is through them that the sacred powers of the Universe flow.

Reconnection Through Myth And Story

In the stories of the Druid tradition there is a wealth of wisdom and knowledge. Not only gods and goddesses can be found in the stories, but innerworld teachers such as Merlin, Taliesin and the Otherworldly women, such as the Ladies of the Lake in the Arthurian tales, who work in the service of the Goddess and the land. Heroes who protect the land and guard the gateways. Goddesses who challenge the seeker of the mysteries of life, to change and grow. They are all here in the stories and also rooted deep within our unconscious, ready to re-awaken like the legendary King Arthur when the earth has need. Well, the earth has need and the life of the earth has need. Whether we live within the shores of Britain or in a land beyond its waves, the voices of the old gods will be heard when it is our time to come home. This does not of course, require that we travel from the four corners of the earth to make our home in the lands of the Celts, it means that we come home to ourselves, to our deep and whole self. We can begin by listening to the voices of our ancestors in the stories of King Arthur and his court, or the older tales of the Mabinogian, Cerridwen and Taliesin, Cullowch and Olwen and a host of others. There has been so much wonderful work done with these stories in recent years. Many more manuscripts that have lain for hundreds of years in dusty vaults have yet to be translated from the old languages.

Druids As Ecology

When we come to know the earth as sacred then conservation and ecologically sound management of the earth's resources follow as a matter of course. Living in harmony with the earth is a way of life in Druidry. Whether we are recycling glass bottles or working as an environmental scientist, we can all help in our own way. Druidryand all those who practice it are committed to working, either as individuals or collectively, towards a more ecologically *sustainable* environment. The earth is our home, but more than that it is the source of our physical existence, our earthly life. We need to take care of it and respect it as a living, nurturing being. The earth is not something that we can take for granted as an endless resource from which we can endlessly take, without giving in return. We can think of it more like a bank account, if we only make withdrawals, sooner or later we are in big trouble. The old idea of having 'dominion over the Earth' has not served us well, it has led to naive and unrealistic expectations that endanger us all. The Earth herself will survive in some way no matter how we behave, even as a dead planet. It is the life of the earth that is threatened and that includes us. The Druidic understanding that the earth is sacred, our home, our mother, is a vital, 'down to earth', 'hands on', empowering way of life.

The planting of broadleaf woodland, or just a single tree, the use of environmentally sound items in the home, such as cleaning fluids and collecting bits of rubbish, such as broken bottles, plastic bags, sweet wrappers, etc., when we walk in the countryside, all helps. Low-energy light bulbs and re-using supermarket carrier bags may *seem* small things, but over a lifetime they will help enormously.

Remember: 'Think Globally, Act Locally'.

PRACTICE

Read whatever you can about the gods and goddesses who 'speak' to you, come to know them and their stories.

But remember you also have your own story, which is just as important. The dragons that we fear in today's world may not resemble those found in legend, well not in looks, but they can feel just as ferocious until we learn how to deal with them.

Whilst you may not see yourself as one of King Arthur's knights, your search for the Grail-will be just as meaningful as it was in the stories of Arthur: Your own birth story was your first initiation in this lifetime, the struggles and the joys you have experienced along your journey are all part of your own unique and scared quest. The ancestors who walked this earth before you will share their wisdom if you get to know them: if your family history is difficult to discover, the ancestors of your greater family, your tribe, your nation will be there for you. The blessings of the Spirits of the natural world are there for you also.

Begin to write your own story; it is the story of one human being's sacred and courageous journey through life. It is the beginning of your barbic work: unless you wish to, you need show no one, but maybe you could leave your story for future generations.

Chapter 7 – Ceremony, Ritual and Magic

I have come *here to search the way,*

To find the red egg;

The red egg of the marine serpent,

By *the sea-side in the hollow of the stone.*

I am going to seek in the valley

The green water-cress, and the golden grass,

And the top branch of the Oak,

In the wood by the side of the fountain.

Lyra Celtica, Merlin the Deviner

What is Ritual?

In the mundane sense putting the cat out, locking the doors, turning the lights out and reading before we go to sleep; when repeated every night all become a ritual, but for now we are going to look at a different sort of ritual.

We are going to look at ritual as a ceremonial act with sacred purpose. These rituals help us to more deeply connect with the forces at work beyond our everyday sense of the world. The Gods, Goddesses, Innerworld Teachers, the Spirits of Time and Place, the Spirits of the Ancestors all can be communicated with through a wisely constructed ritual.

So what do I mean by 'wisely constructed'? Well, in order to travel to a particular distant destination you would need certain information, such as, where is this place? What time does the train or bus leave? You know the sort of thing. Ritual is, in a sense just the same, you need information and the ability to make good use of that information. These skills you can learn. You then need to combine these skills with integrity, passion, humility and humor. Althoughwe can be absolutely serious about what we do, it is unwise to take ourselves too seriously and believe we can command the Universe to do our bidding and serve our personal needs. We can't! If we try, we are only setting ourselves up to learn a *big* lesson in arrogance. We can work in dynamic harmony with the power of the Universe, but to think that we can change its course safely is a fool's notion.

Humor and humility are essential. Humor does not mean making fun of what is being done in the ritual, it means taking lightly anything that apparently seems like a mistake; remember you are connecting with 'unseen' forces, they may just be intervening. Humor also means enjoying what you do, finding the joy in it. It's of no use to take part in ritual if you do it grudgingly or it seems like a chore. Humility does not mean feeling like a worthless, subservient thing, asking the powers that be to give us what we want, or to change our life while we sit back and rest. Ritual is a sacred act through which we can connect with spiritual powers that not only exist in the Universe but also flow through us. So, in order to make changes in our lives, we need to work beyond the ritual and make the necessary changes in the outer world in order for change to take place. When we weave the inner and outer forces together in harmony within our lives and in harmony with the Universe we are truly empowered.

What Information Do I Need?

In the previous chapters there is a great deal of information to create a ritual for the eight festivals or the four quarters, such as theposition of the elements in the four quarters, for example earth in the north and fire in the south, etc. You also have information on the correspondences of those quarters, for example east is light, birth, air, masculine, etc. But let's collect even more information before we create a ceremony later on in the book.

Ceremony

Ceremony and ritual can, of course, be combined. There are many different ceremonies that we celebrate in Druidry which give an increasing depth of meaning to life. Ceremonies can be as formal or informal as you wish and this depends on all the factors coming together at a particular place and time and on the people involved. Some of the ceremonies in Druidry are wild, joyous affairs, filled with music, dance, costume and laughter, while others are the silent offering of thanks to the spirits of those who guide us. Some ceremonies are well structured with the participants taking specific roles, others are spontaneous expressions of that which flows through the ceremony.

Ceremonies are used to celebrate the eight festivals of the Druid year and are seen as times when we can connect to the turning wheel of the year and our own natural cycles. There are ceremonies which are performed as initiations into another aspect of life and celebrate a deeper connection with and a growing understanding of that particular aspect. Some of these initiations are known as rights of passage and honor our life's journey through birth, puberty, the middle years and death. Initiations also take place in some Druid orders when a new Bard is welcomed into the group and makes a commitment to their spiritual path. Later as they begin to work as an Ovate, they will take an initiation that serves as a gateway to the wisdom of the Ovates. The same process will happen when they move into the work of the Druid or Druidess. So we can understand rites of passage as sacred gateways, each gateway created through knowledge, ceremony and ritual.

Magic

This is a huge subject and the space we have only allows us to touch upon it. Magic dates back to the earliest times of our human story. In the cave paintings of our ancestors we can speculate that the hunting scenes are acts of magic where the shaman is connecting with the spirits of the animals to bring about success in the hunt and therefore providing food and life for the tribe. In later times, we find evidence of ritual sacrifices being offered to the gods in exchange for the troubled life of the people. These were sacred and magical acts made in times of great need. Sacrifice means to 'make sacred'. This form of magic is thankfully no longer practiced. Magical acts today have one sacrosanct law which all pagans whether Druid, Wiccan or any other responsible Pagan group uphold, Thou shall harm none'. This law is clear and unambiguous and, ideally, means in thought, word, deed. This law does, of course, extend beyond a magical ritual and into our everyday life.

Magic is usually practiced through ritual, when the forces of the Otherworlds are called upon to work with the practitioner's will, in order to create a specific change in the world, in the physical world or in consciousness. Magic ranges from folk spells, through healing to the high magic of mystical union with deity. Magic should never interfere with another human being against their will. Even healing magic should have the permission of the person who is sick. Integrity is absolutely essential in magic.

A magical act should never be performed unless *all* the consequences have been taken into consideration. Which, in reality, is a tall order as human beings only have limited vision and the 'magician' must accept full responsibility for the outcome! If in doubt, don't do it.

As you can see ceremony, ritual and magic are not clearly defined. Magic is a ritual act, ceremony can be also ritualistic and a ceremony can also be magical. In Druidry rather than performing 'spells' to bring about change, we focus on making changes in our life through study, meditation, therapy, ritual, ceremony and discussion, which allow the changes to take place in our consciousness. Druidry is a path of living *consciously* in the world and through connecting with Druidry's growing wisdom we can increasingly expand our consciousness allowing us greater choice and power in our lives. Until we have a greater mastery of our own lives through wisdom, insight and compassion, magic can be at best ineffectual and at worst harmful, no matter how good the intention.

The Mechanics Of Ceremony And Ritual

We already have a lot of the necessary information, now let's look at the 'mechanics' of ceremony. It is here that we start to weave it all together and the starting point is the circle. As we have seen, the circle symbolizes many things; the whole non-dualistic self, the cosmos, the wheel of the year and now, in ceremony it is defining the sacred space in which we work. Later, if it feels right, you can decide just what your ceremony will be for, but for now we will create a general idea of the mechanics.

Casting The Circle

In order to define our space we bring together the skills and information we have already gathered. Interwoven around the wheel of the year are the masculine and feminine principles of life, seen in the four solar festivals and the four fire festivals. We can correlate these principles with golden and silver light, respectively. These principles are part of each one of us and also flow through the Universe and in casting the circle we are calling upon these powers in visualization, intent and knowledge to create a safe and sacred space in which to work.

Stand in the east, the place of new beginnings. Use whatever of your skills you need to help you relax, then calling upon your ability to visualize and the power and passion of your feelings, extend your arm, whichever one feels right for you, imagine the united powers of the masculine and feminine flowing through you body and travelling down your extended arm and out towards where you sense the eastern point of your circle lies. Remember, this power will be 'seen' as golden and silver light, now begin to walk sunwise around the circle visualizing the golden and silver light forming the boundaries of your sacred space. Continue until you have formed a circle and when you arrive back in the east, the circle is complete. In your own way acknowledge the powers that have created your sacred circle.

Opening The Four Quarters

Now you stand within your circle of light, it is time to call upon the powers that dwell within the four quarters. By this time you have the knowledge of the correspondences of those quarters and it is up to you to invite (not demand) into your circle whatever you feel is appropriate. Ask for the blessings of these powers. Standing in the east and facing out towards the east, you may wish to say something like this:

'I stand in the east, in the place of first light and I call upon the

powers of air and clarity to bless this circle with their presence.'

Once again use your powers of visualization, feeling and focus to invoke the blessings of the east.

Then walk to the south, take your time, be aware of your feet upon the earth, every step you take is a sacred step upon the earth. Using knowledge, visualization, feeling and focus call upon the powers of the south. Again ask for their blessings, try and keep a flowing pattern to your invocations, about the same length and structure. For instance:

'I stand in *the south* in *the place of the sun's greatest light and I call upon the powers of fire and inspiration to bless this* circle *with their presence.'*

Now walk to the west, summoning all your skills and call upon the powers of the west. A flowing pattern may go:

'I stand in *the west,* in *the place of the setting sun and I call upon the powers of water and intuition to bless this* circle *with their presence.'*

Then on to the north, standing facing out to the northern quarter, you may say for example:

'I stand in *the North,* in *the place of greatest darkness and I call upon the powers of earth and steadfastness to bless this* circle *with their presence.'*

Turn to the center and ask the spirit of the circle to bless your ceremony.

You have now created a very special place in which to work, it is a sacred space. Your circle is blessed by the powers of god and goddess, light and dark, the four elements and the powers of inspiration, intuition, steadfastness and clarity. The spirit of the circle blesses your work and you are ready to begin.

Let's go through a few points:

1 Your circle can be used for meditation, ceremony, ritual, healing, etc.

2 You can work indoors or outdoors.

3 Always choose a time when you will be uninterrupted. If indoors, un-plug the telephone, a sudden interruption can be quite a shock if you are deep in meditation.

4 Before you cast the circle, take into your chosen space everything that you will need for your ceremony. Once the circle is cast try not to leave it until you have finished, unless you really must. If the house catches fire or if you are outdoors and a herd of stampeding cattle are heading towards you ... leave!

5 If it is not appropriate for you to create a 'physical' circle, then create the whole thing in meditation; imagine yourself going through the sequence of events just as you would do in the physical world.

6 Always give yourself plenty of time, so that you can relax and have *no* need to keep one eye on the clock.

Closing The Circle

Whether in meditation or as a physical ceremony, the need to close a circle well is as important as opening it well. As we have seen, our work in the circle connects us with the powers of the Otherworlds and while we can understand that all the Worlds touch and in a sense flow through one another, it is absolutely vital that outside the circle, we make *conscious* the boundaries between the physical world and the world of Spirit. Whatever your work is about in meditation or ceremony, opening and closing the circle clearly and firmly can be thought of as the 'take off' and 'landing' of an airplane. A crash landing can be very uncomfortable. If we don't 'close down' properly, a sense of feeling 'spaced out' can be very unpleasant and if you are driving soon afterwards, can also be dangerous! It can lead to very confused dreams and to lose a conscious distinction between the worlds is the path to psychological illness. If you are going to work with altered states of consciousness there are dangers *unless* you follow well researched guidelines. Whilst the dangers are sometimes inflated into the realms of the ridiculous, make good use of your common sense. Headaches and spacyness are unpleasant and can be avoided.

If you are taking any form of medication that affects your consciousness, check with your doctor before you go ahead. Ask him or her if they think that meditation is suitable for you.

If you have been suffering from a psychological illness, either now or in the past, working with altered states of consciousness may well not be appropriate for you. In this instance **ALWAYS** check with your doctor or therapist and **DO** take their advice. There are many other ways to work in Druidry, the work we have just discussed is only a small part of it. Remember your spiritual path is a journey to wholeness, not fragmentation.

Now the mechanics of closing down the circle. In either ceremony or meditation we simply reverse the process of opening the circle.

Don't rush, it's important.

Stand in the east, facing the center of the circle and, in your own words, thank the Spirit of the circle for its presence and its blessings. Now walk to the north, in the *opposite* direction to the path of the sun. Stand facing outwards and again, using your powers of visualization, intent and focus, plus your heart and the feelings of being truly blessed, in your own words thank the powers of the north for their blessings and their presence. Let the images of your visualization gently fade until you are looking at your physical surroundings in the north. When the 'inner' images have cleared walk to the west and then the south and finally to the east, repeating the same process. You are now going to open the circle of golden and silver light. Visualize the circle of light and once again, extend your arm until you feel to be 'in contact' with the circle. In your own words thank the God and the Goddess for their presence and their blessings and begin to walk around the circle, once again in the opposite direction to the path of the sun, letting the image of golden and silver light gently fade until you stand once more in the east. You may like to turn to the center and say something like:

'I now declare this circle open in the physical world, may the

physical world be blessed.'

Feel yourself fully present in the physical world, stretch your body, feel at home in it, with your feet firmly on the earth. Now have something to eat (a couple of biscuits would be fine) and drink, maybe something warm, you may feel a little chilled and a warm drink will help.

And finally, well done, brilliant! You have now woven together all the skills that you have been patiently developing throughout this book. Let them grow with added knowledge and insight, giving a rich and joyous dimension to your life and a deeper connection with 'all that is'.

Unless there are specific reasons for doing otherwise, whenever you move around in your circle during the ceremony, always take the path of the sun. This regular sunwise movement helps to create a vortex of energy that will help give power to your ceremony. Only in the final closing down period do you need to walk in the opposite direction, thus helping to earth the sometimes-powerful energy that has been built up.

Ceremony And The Eight Festivals

Because of our conscious relationship with the world of nature, Druids around the world celebrate the eight festivals of the year outdoors whenever we can. It is a way of honoring the natural world that helps us attune to the changing seasons and the elements. To stand beneath the starry heavens on a clear frosty night, listening to the haunting call of an owl and the crackle of the fire that burns within the center of the circle; to smell the sweet scent of wood smoke on the wind and feel the presence of spirits of the trees is a magical part of our lives. At the dawn of the summer solstice, as we welcome the first rays of light as the sun begins its ascent from eastern horizon, we cannot help but feel that magic is alive in the world and that we are part of that magic.

However you choose to celebrate the festivals, whether alone orwith friends, you now have much of the information you will need to help attune your own life to that of the world of nature. If youchoose to celebrate in a public place remember that you are not putting on a public performance, it is a sacred celebration and you may feel more at ease working with a degree of privacy. Some Druid Orders do, of course, celebrate in public areas and if you are around at the time, ask if you can join in. Always ask permission if you would like to celebrate on land that doesn't belong to you. Many large landowners such as the National Trust and English Heritagein Britain will be very willing as long as you let them know of your intentions and respect any guidelines they issue.

Create your ceremony in whatever way feels right for you, takinginto consideration all that you have read so far, it can be as simple or as complex as you wish. Share food with one another, readstories; send your blessing to the spirits of the animals, the trees, the rivers and the land. Most importantly, enjoy it.

PRACTICE – Creating A Ceremony

At whatever time of the year you are reading this, check to see which festival you are approaching and begin to plan a ceremony that incorporates a clearly constructed ritual. You may find that you cannot carry it out in practice, the but the act of creating it will also help you attune and you could go through it in meditation at the appropriate time. Following is a list of the festivals, their dates and some correspondences that will help you. The dates apply to the Northern Hemisphere so if you are in the Southern Hemisphere, the date that applies to the ceremony across the circle.

Imbolc – 2 February – the goddess Brighid, snowdrops, water, candles, new tender shoots of spring growth, all new life.

Alban Eiler – 21 March – youth, spring and the greening earth, a time of balance, day and night are equal.

Bealtainne – 1 May – fire, sexuality, potency, may blossom, the vibrant life of the earth.

Alban Heruin – 21 June – the longest day, the greenest light, sunflowers, gold, creativity manifest in the world.

Lughnasadh – 1 August – the beginning of the harvest, heat, corn, the sun god Lugh, the wheel.

Alban Elued – 21 September – the autumn equinox, the rich crops of the harvest, the seed, the gold/red leaves of autumn, the dying sun.

Samhuinn – 31 October – Honouring the ancestors, letting go, the death of the old year, the Celtic new year, the Calleach as the goddess of winter and death.

Alban Arthuan – 21 December – the birth of the Mabon, the shortest day, the germinating seeds in the womb of the earth.

There is so much more to be added to this very short list, but you can spend the rest of your life discovering what each festival means to you.

Chapter 8 – Straight Time, Curved Time

So simple is the earth we tread,

So quick with love and life her frame,

Ten thousand years have dawned and fled,

And still her magic is the same.

Stopford A. Brooke, The Earth and Man

Life As Linear Time

The dynamics of work in the circle and therefore your understanding of life as cyclic and whole, are completely different from the dynamics of life as it is understood in linear time. When we work with linear time, past, present and future follow one another as though along a straight line and we are continually leaving all that has gone before. Past and future never meet, they are seen as separate and discrete. We are born, we live and then we die, we cease to exist. It can be a very frightening concept. The past has gone and we can bury all our pains, move on and never have to look at them again. But this doesn't explain how life really feels.

Whatever we hope that we might have buried along this longstraight road has a nasty habit of turning up at the mostinconvenient times and throwing us off balance. We cannot in a sense leave the past; it is part of our root system. As we gain a growing understanding of all that we have experienced in life, good and bad, and are able to draw wisdom from it, we begin to provide a fertile ground for our future growth. Life can be a very tough journey, and many times we cannot bear to look back on the pains that we have suffered. But when we try to bury them and, sometimes, through great need we are very successful, we may just be burying our greatest treasures also. So, through no fault of our own, our unique and special gifts never see the light of day. I say *through* no *fault of our own,* because unless we are taught the skills to deal with life, we simply do the best we can.

The understanding gained in working with the circle in ceremony and ritual through the turning wheel of the year, helps us to develop the wisdom and the skills to safely clear the painful debris of our past and release the wonderful gifts that help ourselves and others to live life more fully. A sound and growing connection rooted deep in the world of nature provides an anchor point from which we can safely explore ourselves. Connection with both the masculine and feminine aspects of Deity can give us a real sense of being loved, unconditionally loved. The Gods and Goddesses of the Druid tradition are not judgmental beings ready to banish us into damnation because we have failed in some way. Instead they offer us wisdom and the ability to feel strong enough to make great changes in the way we approach life. Through a cyclic understanding of life they offer us new perspectives from where we can see that wherever sorrow is, joy is also present; wherever light is, darkness is also present; wherever death is, life is also present.

The apparent opposites of life can be better understood as complementary. When we view life and death, etc., as opposites we are in a sense viewing life through a linear understanding. Life is at one end of the line and death at the other. Opposition gives the sense of two forces in conflict with one another, like warring armies when only one side can win. If that is how we view life then that is exactly how it will feel.

Life As Cyclic Time

Now let's look at life through an understandingof cyclic time and for now we will use the word 'complementary'instead of the word 'opposite'. By now you have a strong sense of the wheel of the year and its importance in Druidry. When you look at the illustration of the wheel, you will find that across the circle from the summer solstice, the time of greatest light is the winter solstice, the time of greatest darkness. They exist as complementary to one anotheracross the circle and across the spectrum of time. Without the knowledge of darkness we would have no sense of the light. Across the circle from noon is midnight, without the knowledge of nighttime we would have no sense of the day. Across the circle from the Maiden, is the Wise-Woman; across the circle from the Bright Mother of Bealtainne, is the Dark Mother, the Crone of Samhuinn. And so it goes, from whichever point of the circle you view life, its complement is always present and with insight, its influence can be detected. In the west is the place of autumn and the setting sun, the gateway to physical death, just as the sun dies to us each evening. But it is not the *end* of the sun, in the east it will be reborn in the place of new beginnings the following dawn. So as you stand in the west in the place of the gateway that leads beyond this world, across the circle, but still *within and part of the circle,* is the gateway to new life. When the Northern Hemisphere is bathed in daylight, the Southern Hemisphere is resting in the silent darkness. When Druids in the Southern Hemisphere are celebrating Bealtainne, Druids in the Northern Hemisphere are celebrating Samhuinn. It is the way of the natural order of things in our physical world, where one thing is present; its complementary is also present but may be hidden from our view. And it is the view we have of life that dictates whether we feel empowered to really live fully in the world or feel like a pawn in some vast game that we have no say in. As we have seen the circle represents the self, the whole self, every bit of us, our pains, our joys, our anger, our inspiration, everything. When we know ourselves to be an integral part of the greater circle of life and it too has its darkness, its joy, its stillness and its wildness, then we can understand ourselves to be no longer alone, we are part of the rich joyous dance of life. We are part of everything there is and we can work in a profound relationship with life.

Working With The knowledge Of The Circle

Imagine yourself at a time in your life when you feel trapped, with nowhere to turn. Everything seems dark and you no longer feel the joy of life. Life feels stagnant and dead. Maybe you won't need to *imagine* how this feels, you may be experiencing these feelings right now! Look at the wheel and see where your feelings would fit in the greater scheme of things. As you will find, it is at the time of the winter solstice when the sun's warmth has left us and the nights are long and cold, the time of greatest darkness. The winter solstice is situated in the north, the place of earth and stillness. The spirits of place and time come together and through them is born that part of the year we know as the winter solstice. In just the same way the spirits of time and place, our own time in the world and our own particular place in our life's journey and produce the feelings of cold, darkness, stagnation, rigidity, loneliness, sorrow, depression. It may happen around the time of the winter solstice, but not necessarily, it will be just at the right time for each one of us. Unless we can understand these feelings as part of the experience of being human and part of the natural order of things and how we can work *with* them, it can be an overwhelmingly lonely time in our lives. So how does the knowledge of the circle help? One of the things that we have seen is that, in the natural order of things, there is one dynamic that we can be sure of and that is change. All things in the Universe are in a continual state of change and when we try and fight this change it can be a very painful experience, for we are in essence trying to fight the laws of the Universe and the deeper needs of our soul. It takes a great deal of energy to maintain a static position when confronted by the powers of the Universe! But of course we all try and do it at sometime in our life and when we do it simply adds to the feelings that we see depicted in the wheel at the time of the winter solstice. We lose all our energy, it feels like death and in the darkness there is no way of seeing how to make any changes. But if we want things to change, how can we be resisting change? As we saw earlier, we all have buried deep within our unconscious thoughts, patterns, habits, sorrows that we would rather leave buried and we have usually done an expert job of burying them until even our conscious self can no longer see them. Now, this is where the true magic of Druidry comes in! Look againat the winter solstice, it is a time when the earth rests. When we learn to let go and trust a deeper part of ourselves, we can also rest; at this time there is no need to fight for change. If you need to sleep, then sleep. Consciously let go, allow yourself to be in harmony with the earth and rest. Look again at the wisdom of the winter solstice; the seeds of the past are already germinating deep within the dark cold earth, ready to produce a new season's growth when the time is right. The seeds fell from the crops, which were part of the dyingyear, fertilized by the rotting vegetation that supported the growth of those crops. You also have the seeds of change deep within you and if you take time to rest, they may just surface in your dreamworld or as insights in your waking life. Simply relax, you may read just what you need to know in a book, or a friend says something thatconnects you to the hidden seeds that will grow into a new way of thinking and acting in the world ... when the time is right. All that is now superfluous to your journey through life, the very things that you began to recognize at the previous festival of Samhuinn will, as you allow them to become more fully conscious, become that which 'fertilizes' the seeds of change. Look once more at the winter solstice, it is the time of the birth of the Mabon, the sun child, the self. You are beginning to let the greater wisdom of your whole self be born into the world, with all its glory, all its life and power and potential. It is very precious, cherish it, nourish it, give it space to grow into your earthly life. For it is the wise prompting of the self needing to be born into the world that we are responding to when we begin our search for greater meaning in life. Across the circle from this dark time in your life is the brilliant light of the sun in its splendor, in full and glorious union with the Earth. It is you, in your full and potent self, fully awake and alive in the world. It will be born from the sacred darkness of the womb of the Earth Mother. Through the turning circle of life through the teachings of the Druid tradition we can attain the wisdom and the skills to be *fully* present upon the earth and in this state we are truly healed and whole.

This journey of course lasts throughout our lives. In Druidry there is no quick fix, it is a continuing journey of self-discovery that is rooted into the very fabric of life.

PRACTICE

You may like to try this simple but stunning experiment. If you are familiar with the color wheel through your understanding of art, you may have already tried this, it is pure magic. White light contains within it a whole spectrum of colors, which through our sense of sight we can see as the colors of the rainbow. Theyeach have their own wave frequency, the longest and slowest being the color red. Then a little shorter and faster is orange,then yellow, green, blue, violet and finally Indigo, giving the seven frequencies that we can detect with the naked eye as color. Just as we have come to view life as cyclic rather than linear. we can best understand these colors when they form a circle rather than a straight line. In this form, green will lie across the circle from red; blue will lie across the circle from orange; and violet will lie across the circle from yellow.

Each pair, red and green, blue and orange, yellow and violet are known as complementary colors, they lie at either end of that particular spectrum of color. They complement one another, where one is, the other is present also, but apparently unseen to our ordinary vision. Now this, of course, sounds very similar to our experience of the wheel of the year and therefore of life. This is the power of Druidic teaching, its wisdom comes not from 'one' person's vision of life, but from life itself. The more we look at life in the natural world, observe its cycles, its changes and its *apparent* opposites we come to realize that all life is one great living dynamic being and we are an integral part of it. Nothing is truly separate; separateness is simply how we tend to experience life until we learn to widen our perspective. Things needn't oppose one another when we can see them as complementary aspects contained within the whole. To come to the realization that life and death are present within each other, that joy and sorrow are found in the same place we need a different view than a linear perspective offers us. We can in time, through working with the knowledge of the circle come to that empowering and liberating understanding. But in order to see a little of this truth for yourself, try this experiment.

Take a sheet of unlined white paper and a colored pen or paint, something that will give you a good bright clear color such as red, blue or green. Draw, approximately, a *10* cm (4 inch) square of your chosen color on to the white paper, fill the square completely with color. You could alternatively cut a 10cmsquare of colored paper and glue it on to the white background. The important thing is that you have a solid block of a single bright color on the white background. Now place it at about the distance away from you that you would normally read a book and focus on the colored square. Make sure you are comfortable; it may take five minutes or more. Don't tire your eyes, soften your focus and continue to look at the square. Eventually, as *if by magic,* its complementary color can be seen shimmering around your square, both ends of the spectrum of your chosen color exist in unison with one another. Where one is present its complement also exists. This truth flows through life, within each one of us whether male or female, the complementary principle exists.

CHAPTER 9 – Life, Death And Rebirth

Three times I have been born,

I know by meditation; Anyone would be foolish not to come and obtain

All the sciences of the world from my breast.

For I know what has been, what in future will occur.

I know all the names of the stars from North to South;

I have been in the galaxy at the throne of the Distributor

I have been three periods in the Prison of Arianrhod...

Taliesin

Reincarnation And Transmigration

The continuing life of the soul as it travels through the worlds, in and out of incarnation has always been a fundamental part of Druidic belief. That we have known many existences as well as our present life and in forms other than human is an essential aspect of spiritual teachings throughout many cultures around the world. For many thousands of years it has been one of the world's great religious themes. Reincarnation is an empowering belief for thousands of people. That there is an undying essential 'something' that flows through time and exists beyond each physical death, is now being scientifically researched.

In 325 CE the Emperor Constantine called the Council of Nicea in order to determine what was 'politically correct' for an Orthodox Christian Church. Reincarnation was definitely not 'p.c.' It challenged the Church's teaching of the resurrection of the body of Christ, which in turn weakened the power of Rome. Origen, one of the early church father's wrote: 'Every soul... comes into this world strengthened by the victories or weakened by the defeats of its previous life'. In the last years of his life he was imprisoned and tortured for his beliefs. Beliefs that until this time were widely held within the Church. Catholic doctrine was going to be just that, catholic! Bishops deviating from the 'politically correct' dogma would be disposed of. The death sentence (ironically) on reincarnation, was issued by the Emperor Justinian following the Synod of Constantinople in 543 CE when he stated: 'If anyone asserts the pre-existence of souls, and shall assert the monstrous restoration which follows from it: let him be anathema (cursed!)'. Justinian obviously wasn't too well versed in Christian charity. Well, as the saying goes, 'reincarnation is making a comeback'. In today's world there are those within the Church who according to theology professor Dr Pascal Kaplan find that an understanding of rebirth 'provides a framework for a deeper, truer understanding of their religion and of the essence of Christian spirituality'.

Reincarnation or transmigration of the soul is interpreted in many ways through many different cultures. Some believing that we move from lesser births as animals, etc. towards more intelligent human beings! In some cultures a definite period of time is said to elapse between births, in others that we can take births in other worlds beyond this realm.

The Dalai Lama has stated that 'It (reincarnation) is related to the theory of interdependent origination ...' This is a vital part of the understanding of rebirth. If everything is of one and the same vast essential being that we witness throughout the manifest world in the life and death cycles of the seasons, in the movement of sub-atomic particles, in the birth and death of stars, then how can we, as human beings be different? Everything in the Universe is in a state of change. From a spinning cloud of gas, our solar system was born, from this original matter sprang all life on earth. Every atom of our physical being was once part of the starry heavens and will eventually go back to the Earth Mother to form other physical forms. That which animates life also moves on, taking many forms on its journey of experiencing the worlds of form and beyond into the formless realms of spirit.

The Circles of Existence

In Druidry today we work with a 'map' of the soul's journey that we name as the circles of existence. Druidry has always held the knowledge of the immortality of the soul. The Irish word *tuirgen* implies a circuit of births in which the soul passes through all possible forms of matter and spirit before it is at one within the realm of Ceugant.

In the writings of the sixth-century poet Taliesin, the 'Primary Chief Bard of Britain' we find testimony to his enlightened knowledge of his own journey through Life:

I have been a cat with a speckled head on three trees

I have been a well-filled crane-bag, a sight to behold.

I am a harmonious one; I am a clear singer;

I am steel, I am a Druid ...

Taliesin

Our journey spans aeons of time and according to Druidry's teachings, begins in the realm of Annwn (pronounced *An-noon),* a sort of cosmic soup, from which all life evolved. From Annwn we journey into the realm of 'life as we know it', this earthly life, the spiralling circles of Abred. Within Abred we experience all forms of life, gaining growing understanding, making mistakes, learning, forgetting and remembering until the light of Gwynvid begins to enter our conscious existence and we begin our search for an enlightened way of living on this earth. Gwynvid means the white life and is the circle of light. In the realms of Abred we experience a life of separation and dualism, of life and death. We can experience isolation from those we love and death seems to separate us beyond bearing. It is in this realm that we begin to sense that we are cut off from something which is absolutely vital to the deeper needs of our soul. Ironically, it is that which we feel cut off from which is calling to us and when we begin our search, we have truly begun our long journey home. This profound moment in a soul's evolutionary journey is the moment when you and I know without question that there is a much deeper meaning to life and nothing is going to stop us finding that meaning. It is the beginning of our personal Grail quest. As T.S. Elliot wrote:

...at the end of all our exploring

Will be to arrive where we started

And know the place for the first time...

Through the many circles and cycles that our soul has endured we suddenly begin to remember who, what and where we are. The Great Mother who gave us form throughout our many incarnations and the Lord of Life who seeded those lives have taught us well and in our turn, we can work with them to help others in the world. The light of Gwynvid begins to illumine our darkness until we dwell beyond Abred in the formless circle of light. Beyond Gwynvid lies the realm of Ceugant, the Great Spirit, the one source of all being.

The Blessed Isles

Between each lifetime, when we pass from this earthly life through the gateway in the west, we leave our physical body behind and in our body of light we travel to the Blessed Isles to rest until it is our time to return to a life on earth. The Blessed Isles lie beyond the realm of our physical sight, but in our inner journeys we may travel there to commune with the ancestral spirits that hold the knowledge that we may need to help us grow and change in harmony with the greater flow of life. There are those in Druidry today who speak more directly with the spirits of the ancestors, reclaiming wisdom that lays buried beneath the rubble of crumbling institutions.

At Samhuinn we invite the spirits of the ancestors to join us for a while in the sacredness of the circle, we share a symbolic feast together and honor the journey that they once made upon this earth. Whatever joys or sorrows their lives held, whatever pains or gifts they left in the world, they were like each one of us; human beings longing to be loved, longing to know their place in the world. Many of them will have returned to this earth, time and time again. Some may very recently have travelled to the Blessed Isles, at the end of the Samhuinn ceremony we wish them well and bid them a safe return to their sacred isle.

In this place we will know no hardship, there is no judgmental God condemning us to a life in purgatory, each soul is a spark of the Great Spirit and therefore knows the lessons it must learn when it returns to earth. The Blessed Isles is a place of transition, where even the innerworld teachers will one day move on from, when there are those souls ready to take on their task. It is a place out of and beyond our experience of time and so Druidry holds no belief in a set number of years or months in which the soul dwells in the Blessed Isles. When the time is right, we move on.

The Mabon And The Goddess

The Mabon holds a special place in my heart; it speaks to me of many things and holds both joy and sorrow in its pure clear light. The Mabon can be understood as the self, that divine spark of the one pure light, which is the source of each one of us. The Mabon is born at the time of greatest darkness from the womb of the Earth Mother, at the time of the winter solstice. It corresponds to the moment when each soul is born into the apparent darkness of earthly life. But rebirth into the world is far from being a 'fall from grace'. The soul is born from the womb of the goddess and it is through her in all earthly forms, whether we are male or female, that we come to know the wisdom of the earth. The following quote from Tsultrim Allione's book 'Women of Wisdom', applies to each one of us when we allow the divine feminine a respected and honored place in our lives:

> *The work of woman is transformation: making something out of nothing, giving form to formless energy. Her instruments are the tripod and the Cauldron, her elements blood and milk, both liquids held within her are organic, that with which one works. She is both container and contained at this stage. She transforms matter and is herself transformed. She is the procession of the form and the form of the process.*

The way in which we work with the divine feminine will be different, depending on whether we are male or female, but work with her we must. She is the source of our earthly life and it is through the sacred union of spirit and matter that we will bring to birth the Mabon that lies imprisoned behind the seemingly impenetrable walls of material existence.

The Gods Of Druidry

We have looked a great deal at the divine feminine and how her earthly wisdom flows through all Druidic understanding, but what of the divine masculine? His potency energizes and activates life on earth. Without his fiery presence matter would lay inert, the earth would become a wasteland. When we look around us in the natural world we are witnessing the fruit of the union of God and Goddess. Where we see the Goddess, the God is also present; where we see the God, the Goddess is also present. Their relationship changes and flows through all life as we have seen in the turning seasons of the year. At the time of the winter solstice, from the darkness of her womb, he is born as the sun child. At this time she is the powerful energizer of life. At the time of the summer solstice he is in his full power as energizer of life. He is her life, she is his power. All life on earth is born from their sacred union. Just as the Goddess takes many forms, so too does the God. The Mabon and the sun god Lugh we have already looked at, but two other forms of the God are particularly meaningful in Druidry, Cernnunos and the Green Man. Cernnunos is the wild lord, the powerful, exciting wild energy wefeel in the world of nature. He is the lord of the animals and the wild forests. He is the feeling of Bealtainne, potent sexuality, driving energy, the power of life coursing through our bodies. His magic is beautiful and wild. No wonder the Church turned him into a devil! His dynamic energy must have been too much to handle if you simply wanted to focus on being spiritual. But this is *not the focus* of Druidry. The focus of Druidry is the fruit of the union of this wild, wondrous creative power with the nurturing, forming, sensual power of the Goddess. The focus of Druidry is the healing of the separation between masculine and feminine, between matter and spirit; the focus is the Mabon that dwells within each one of us, waiting to be born into the world.

When I think of the Green Man he makes me smile, with the sort of contentment that I feel after making love. He is the precious power of the masculine completely at one with the feminine. Honoring her, dwelling as equal within her body, he illustrates the love that exists in the natural world, the love that

is shared between God and Goddess. In images we see of the Green Man he dwells at one with nature, his face is seen entwined with the growth of the trees and the foliage of the verdant earth. The green life of the earth sprouts from his mouth and his head; he is entwined with his lover for the entire world to see. This is no judgmental God, but an image of the masculine that we as women long for, a power that the world longs for. Within the Lord of the Wild and the Green Man is the power of the masculine that we have been denied for centuries. But the world can wait no longer, the Goddess calls to Her God and he is answering. May their sacred union be blessed within each one of us.

Printed in Great
Britain
by Amazon